SHATTERED SHELTERED & Strengthened

ONE WOMAN'S TESTIMONY OF HOPE, FORGIVENESS, AND REDEMPTION

GG COX

Published by Innovo Publishing, LLC
www.innovopublishing.com
1-888-546-2111

Publishing Books, eBooks, Audiobooks, Music, Screenplays, & Courses for the Christian & wholesome markets since 2008.

SHATTERED, SHELTERED & STRENGTHENED
One Woman's Testimony of Hope, Forgiveness, and Redemption

Copyright © 2023 by GG Cox
All rights reserved.

No part of this publication may be reproduced, stored in a retrieval system, or transmitted in any form or by any means electronic, mechanical, photocopying, recording, or otherwise, without the prior written permission of the Author.

All personal names have been changed to protect the privacy of individuals. While the story is true, context and details about family, friends, and others have been changed to avoid causing discord while still allowing readers to benefit from the biblical truths in the story.

Unless otherwise noted, all scripture is taken from the King James Version of the Bible. Public domain.

All scripture marked "NLT" is taken from the Holy Bible, New Living Translation, copyright © 1996, 2004, 2015 by Tyndale House Foundation. Used by permission of Tyndale House Publishers, Inc., Carol Stream, Illinois 60188. All rights reserved.

ISBN: 978-1-61314-889-1

Cover Design & Interior Layout: Innovo Publishing, LLC

Printed in the United States of America
U.S. Printing History
First Edition: 2023

Has God called you to create a Christ-centered or wholesome book, eBook, audiobook, music album, screenplay, or online course? Visit Innovo's educational center (cpportal.com) to learn how to accomplish your calling with excellence.

Dedication

This book is dedicated to my three heavenly angels: my mother who trained me, my grandmother who raised me, and my great aunt who prayed for me. It is because of the strength, self-awareness, and sanctification that you each possessed that I am who I am today. *I love and miss you.*

To my daughters: this book is also dedicated to both of you. I pray that I have been both a godly example and spiritual mentor for you. The Lord knows that most of my choices and actions were for you and your protection. Never think that my role as your mother was taken lightly. It is my greatest accomplishment. *I love you both.*

To my husband: if it were not for you, my story would not be what it is, and for that I am both honored and grateful. You gave me the courage to write this book. You have helped make me the woman I am today. It is clear that I was supposed to be your wife. This book is a testament of God's power, healing, and deliverance. This is my story, and I chose to write it to usher in my complete healing and acknowledge the voice and calling God has given to me. I want you to know that I *thank you* for who you are and who you have been in my life. I'm not bitter, but I'm better; I'm not a victim, but I'm victorious; I'm no longer shattered but sheltered and walking in the strength of God. *I forgive and love you.*

I dedicate this book to my two spiritual moms. One is resting in heaven and the other, you know who

DEDICATION

you are. I know it was not easy for you to see me hurt and in pain, but you both loved and carried me all the way through. Today, I still feel your prayers and hear your words. *I love you both.*

To my home church family: *thank you* for the teachings and the many opportunities you gave me to work in the kingdom of God. For the numerous prayers, words of encouragement, and inspiration you spoke into my life. It will never be forgotten. *I love you.*

Lastly, I dedicate this book to my present church family. *Thank you* for being a part of my journey. *Thank you* for loving and respecting the Christ in me. You allowed me to be me and helped push me to walk in my purpose. *I love you.*

Meditation

It was through this season of bitterness, darkness, confusion, shattering, and sheltering that my faith in God grew. My prayer life was strengthened. I learned to walk in purpose and was developed in my calling. Truthfully, this season was dark and ugly. I cannot find enough words to describe all the things I endured. The only way I made it through is the awesome, magnificent, faithful, loving, all-knowing God. From the foundation of the world, before my very existence, God chose me and equipped me to endure this hardness as a good soldier. This is my testimony. You may not understand, agree with, or read beyond this point. And that is

DEDICATION

OK. As a woman of God, I desire every single day of my life to encourage and inspire other women in difficult marriages. I desire for these women to acknowledge and own their story. Never be ashamed of your past marital state. Celebrate the cocoon you have broken out of. Allow God to do His will in and through you. My hope is that other women would be there to pray for, cover, strengthen, and support other women who are weak in their season of despair and brokenness. The Bible tells us in Luke 22:32, "But I have prayed for thee, that thy faith fail not: and when thou art converted, strengthen thy brethren."

Introduction

Have you ever loved, respected, and covered someone who caused you so much hurt, pain, and embarrassment? I'm talking about the person you vowed to be one with—your husband, your covering. The Bible commands, "Husbands, love your wives, just as Christ also loved the church and gave his life for it" (Ephesians 5:25). This scripture describes a man who would do anything to protect his wife. Think about this: a husband should protect and shield his wife from whatever and whomever tries to bring her harm. Be it physically or emotionally, he is there to block it! I know I am not the first nor will I be the last woman scorned and made to feel worthless. I have been cheated on what feels like my entire marriage. From day one, the devil himself made it his personal mission to destroy my marriage. The perplexing thing is, it was not by the hands of a "so-called" friend or foe. The devil was given spiritual authority, all legal rights, and open access to kill, steal, and ultimately destroy our marriage. No one ever dreams their husband, the one you have entrusted with your heart, your spiritual covering and protector, the one who is supposed to love you unconditionally, would ever mistreat you. What's worse, he is a Jesus-loving, sanctified preacher! He chose me because he wanted a Jesus-loving, sanctified woman of God. It should have made a difference!

I grew up in a single-parent home with the help of my maternal grandparents and extended family. I never thought I would meet the man of my dreams,

INTRODUCTION

who would sweep me off my feet and propose to me, and we would live happily ever after. I grew up seeing marriages that withstood heartache and disappointment. Never in a million years did I think I would marry a preacher. He also desired to be a pastor and was installed as such shortly after we married. Our marriage from the beginning was offensive and very toxic. The turbulence I experienced in my marriage has truly been a Lifetime Movie Network series. Yes, I am still married. We have been married now for more than thirty years.

Before you talk about me, judge me, or close this book, I ask you to continue reading my story of heartache, disappointment, and betrayal. More importantly, I want you to read my testimony of faith, compassion, understanding, and healing. There I was, seventeen years old, sitting in church on a Sunday morning. I grew up in a conservative, charismatic church; there was hand clapping, foot stomping, tongue talking, and the laying on of hands in almost every service. This Sunday was like all the other Sundays. I really loved my church. Missionary James, a very fiery, expressive, sanctified missionary, would always lead us in praise and worship. This lasted a good thirty to forty-five minutes. I really miss those days. She would sing multiple songs, play her tambourine, and testify. Depending on the mood and tone of the service, others would testify. If service was high, we did not get out until around three in the afternoon. I can remember like it was yesterday. The Spirit of God came in and blessed us. The pastor came to the podium and encouraged us. He introduced a young preacher from a nearby college who would be the speaker that Sunday. We knew the young preacher must have been a good speaker because our pastor did not allow many preachers behind his podium, especially on a Sunday morning.

The pastor told us that after the choir finished singing, "The next speaking voice would be that of Minister Titus Christopher Lawrence." Needless to say, Minister Titus Christopher allowed God to use him, and the Lord blessed! Minister Titus Christopher prayed, preached, and prophesied. The church enjoyed his ministry. He was young, vibrant, charismatic, and nice looking. And he was single! That Sunday would not be his last time he would be speaking at my church. Minister Titus Christopher became well acquainted with my pastor. During this time, I would see him often, although we never held a conversation. He was in college, and I was in high school. I had not yet committed to the Lord, so he never sparked my interest to introduce myself or communicate with him.

Two years later, I eventually met Minister Titus Christopher through a mutual friend. I never knew his first name, so I didn't know it was him on the other end of the phone. That was a life-changing phone call. After the phone call, we decided to meet in person. I got serious about my relationship with God and, four years later, we were married. Warning really does come before destruction! Reflecting back, I see where the Lord was warning me and giving me insight into my husband's behavior, sexual appetite, and insecurities. I prayed . . . I promise I did. And I heard God's approval for this marriage. Although I never dreamed of marriage, I also never thought about divorce either. Did I have grounds for a divorce? Absolutely!

Meditation

God is saying you will feel the hurt, you will get wounded, you will feel betrayal and shame. But that is not where your story is going to end. Because "no weapon formed against you shall prosper!" God will move you from hurt to healed, sad to soaring, disappointed to deliverance. And broken to blessed. Lift up your eyes, and put your heart in God's hands. Meditate on God's promises, and get ready for a supernatural PUSH. God will show you why they had to do what they did—it did not happen to you; it happened for you! He is going to use what they meant for your harm to elevate you. He is going to bless you right in front of the same people who tried to break you. He will make your enemy your footstool, and he will defend your honor.

Chapter 1

GENERATIONAL CURSES

What is a generational curse? A generational curse is defined as a negative pattern developed from your nuclear family, either on your maternal or paternal side, that is repeated in your life. A few examples of generational curses include marrying an abuser, teen pregnancy, anger and abusive actions, poverty, certain physical or mental issues, idol worshiping, and connecting with certain organizations. When it comes to generational curses, you don't necessarily have to do anything to have a curse attached to you. The Bible declares in Psalms 51:5, "Behold, I was born in sin and shapen in iniquity; and in sin did my mother conceive me." It is at that moment of conception, the seed (zygote, a fertilized egg) is in sin. And that's why it is so important that when a woman becomes pregnant, she covers her child(ren) in prayer, reads the Word of God, and speaks the Word of God over the unborn child(ren). As we begin to age and grow in our nuclear family, there are habits and ideas that become part of us. Some we adopt, and others are just attached to us because of the family we are born into.

Your nuclear family is the family you are born into—your core family (your mom, dad, grandparents, etc.). The nuclear family is where you learn the first of everything. Your nuclear family is responsible for teaching you how to love, how to hate, how to behave in life. From your nuclear family, you learn about social interactions, emotional behavior patterns, spiritual awareness, and the list goes on. I dare not blame all of our bad habits, desires, and patterns on our nuclear family, but when you consider how members in your family have displayed certain behaviors, it is both eye-opening and life-changing. You must be willing to do your own work to be delivered from the curse(s) or sin(s) of your family. These curses and sins manifesting in your life, whether you believe it or not, can affect your loved ones.

I said to do your work. The first step is to acknowledge the curse/sin is there and allow God to do a complete healing in you. *Declare that you will be the one to allow God to break and destroy all generational curses and negative strongholds that have operated and controlled your family for years. Decree it in the name of Jesus!* Job 22:28 says, "Thou shalt also decree a thing, and it shall be established unto thee: and the light shall shine upon thy ways." I am a witness that our awesome God wants to deliver, heal, and set us free from any and all bondage that Satan has orchestrated. He is that kind of God.

The Layer of Revelation

Revelation is a surprising and previously unknown fact. I became aware of generational curses early in my relationship with Christ. After becoming aware of generational curses and understanding how they influence my life, I was shocked. There were things that attached to me just because of who I share blood with, or a last name was revelatory and mind-boggling to say the least. I began to do a self-examination and pray against areas I noticed in my life. I remember how we would just ignore Grandma Daisy when she would say certain things. Or how when a certain person would come around the family during family gatherings, the atmosphere would change. We would go from being happy to see one another to someone almost starting a fight.

The biggest revelation for me was when Uncle John died. Uncle John was the uncle who was around for every party and family reunion, trying to be the gracious host, but in actuality he was known to like his female nieces just a little too much. Not a lot was shared about what he had done, but the little I did hear was enough.

I had to acknowledge some very hard facts about myself and my family history. I believe that once you expose the sin or the curse, you will experience a release. The devil does not like exposure, and the Lord cannot heal what you hide.

Warfare Prayer Is Prayer on Steroids

Warfare is different from praying. Warfare prayer is a time when your prayer is focused on evil and demonic forces that are affecting your daily life and behavior. To go into warfare, your prayer time should be intentional. You must call out every attack of the devil: spiritual, physical, or mental. You must war against evil forces and spiritual strongholds. If you research generational curses in the Bible, you will find several passages of scripture to reflect on. However, there are some writers who don't believe in generational curses. There is limited information in the New Testament concerning the subject:

> Thou shalt not bow down thyself down to them, nor serve them: For I the Lord is a jealous God, visiting the iniquity of the fathers upon the children unto the third and fourth generation of them that hate me. (Exodus 20:5)

> See, I have set before thee this day life and good, and death and evil; I call heaven and earth to record this day against you, that I have set before you life and death, blessings and cursing: therefore choose life, that both thou and thy seed may live. (Deuteronomy 30:15, 19)

Reading these scriptures gives clarity that curses and sins can be passed down through generations. My goal is not to teach on this subject matter; I am only giving more clarity to my personal story. If you trace back the lineage of King David's family, you would see that some of his actions are a direct result of who he came from. This can help you understand some of the consequences that he suffered, but it should also give a whole new meaning for the book of Psalms.

In my prayer and meditation time throughout my marriage, the Lord revealed certain curses and issues that my husband battled with and some my husband allowed to overtake him. During these times, wisdom had to prevail! I could have chosen to confront my husband with this revelational knowledge through embarrassment or belittling, but I knew I was not given this revelation to do that. Instead, I was given the information as a weapon of prayer. I prayed according to Luke 10:19: "Behold, I give unto you power to tread on serpents as scorpions, and over all power of the enemy: and nothing shall by any means hurt you." As wives, we must know that we have the authority to cover our husbands in prayer. Yes, they are our spiritual covering, but wives can and should cover our husbands in prayer. Remember, marriage was ordained by God. Whatever healthy actions you take to preserve your marriage, God will honor. I believe that with all my heart.

The more I prayed for my husband, the more God revealed. (I highly recommend the book *The Power of the Praying Wife* by Stormie Omartian.) For many years, the spirit of perversion was brought prominently to my attention. As I began to research spiritual perversion, I learned better what it means and how it applies to my husband's situation. It is defined as a person's action(s) with deliberate or obstinate desire to behave in a way that is unreasonable or unacceptable often in spite of consequences. Can you see the connection here? One of my husband's generational curses/sin natures came in the area of sexual perversion. Spiritual perversion is directly connected and is both broad and in-depth.

The Layer of Pornography

Pornography is defined as pictures or written material intended to excite an individual sexually. Once in its grip, this stronghold is extremely difficult to be delivered from. It is a *layered* sin. I first became aware of my husband's addiction not long after we were married. We had recently moved to a new state, and I was pregnant and sick most of the time. My husband was the sole provider and took care of everything. We stayed in a busy area of town, and there were a lot of opportunities for entertainment. He came and went as he pleased. Over time, I started to notice how he frequently went in and out of his car trunk.

My husband is a morning person, and he often goes to bed early. I am the opposite. One night, I made it my business to go outside and check the trunk of his car—I wanted to see what he was doing back there. My goodness, there it was! Shocked and confused, I couldn't believe my eyes. If someone had told me he had a porn stash in his trunk, I would have called them a liar. There were books, magazines, and videos. There I was, outside, in the dark, with the trunk wide open. Our bedroom was in the front of the house, and the neighbor's dog was barking. My heart started racing. So nervous about who may walk up on me, I started to sweat. I was appalled and disgusted—sick to my stomach at what I was seeing. I could not believe my husband, this gifted man of God, could be into this. I was frozen, at a complete loss for words, and utterly dumbfounded. All kinds of thoughts started running through my mind: *What else is this man into? Do I really know him? How long has he been looking at this stuff? Was it just because I was pregnant?*

I immediately woke him up to confront him with what I had found. He was very angry and defensive and felt I had completely violated his privacy. That I had no right to snoop through his belongings. I was completely dumbfounded by his reaction. *Are you serious? He has the arrogance to be mad at me? Really?* I hated what I had discovered, and I know he was mortified that I did.

After days of him giving me the silent treatment and being upset with me for finding his stash of porn, he finally opened up and apologized. He shared that he had struggled for a while and that some days were harder than others. I started thinking to myself, *You didn't think this was something I needed to know? You couldn't share this with me before we walked the aisle?* He could not remember when this curse started overtaking him, but he wanted deliverance from it. Reflecting back, I wondered if there were clues that I missed. The only thing I remembered was my husband would watch a movie just to revisit one sex scene. I thought that was strange.

So here we are. What do we do now? The first step was to clean out the junk in the trunk. I helped him tear up every book and magazine, and we smashed every video. If he had more than what was in his trunk, I was never aware of it. We lived in a busy area of town, and there was an adult store right up the road. People could walk in and find everything their hearts desired. It even had a private room where people could watch movies. There were so many options for him beyond the contraband that we destroyed, so I began to hold him accountable. He was uncomfortable of course, but I did not care. I often asked him about his thoughts concerning pornography to see where his head was, and then I reminded him of the Word of God. I would not ridicule him or make judgmental comments, but I would share how I felt.

My husband knew there could never be any of that mess in the house. We stayed away from movies with sex scenes, and I spoke out against all the cable channels that were geared toward sex. There were days, months, even years of fasting and praying for healing and deliverance from pornography. Looking back, we overcame pornography by exposing the sin, faithfully praying, and holding each other accountable. It was extremely challenging. Pornography has many layers, levels, and degrees to it, and although we overcame it, that was just the first crack!

The Layer of Rejection

Rejection is another generational curse my husband has struggled with. It is very deep and very painful to overcome. According to GoodTherapy.org, *rejection* is the dismissal or refusal of a proposal or idea, etc.; similar words are *non-acceptance* or *decline*. My husband has an alpha male complex. Many leaders, including several pastors, display this trait. It was hard initially for me to grasp that rejection is something he struggled with, until I realized that it was a pivotal part of his childhood. As I thought about this more, I realized that there might be a connection between rejection and his pornography struggle. This rejection he felt from family but more so from his peers led him to a lot of loneliness. Being alone, unable to express himself to others, he eventually ventured into pornography as a way to cope with this loneliness.

When we first married, we lived in his hometown, which was about an hour from where I was born, and I would spend a lot of time with his grandmother. I loved and respected her very much and really believed she loved me too. I enjoyed being with her, especially when it was just us, mostly because I missed my grandmother who also raised me. Mother Biggs (and that is exactly what I called her), was a saved and sanctified woman that truly loved God and His children. She was an integral part of my husband's child rearing and was the reason he loved the church and wanted a relationship with God. Mother Biggs was a natural and spiritual mother to many. She shared a lot about my husband's childhood, about his parents' marriage, and how much she prayed for him. I think she shared things with me to try and help me. She wanted me to see why he did certain things and to understand the root issues in his family.

Mother Biggs shared some of the hardships my husband encountered growing up in a small town. He grew up in a family with very little money, and he wasn't given limitless educational opportunities—which others judged him for. He grew up differently from his siblings; he was a special child and experienced ridicule and rejection from not only his peers but from family too. He knew early that he was not like most little boys. He knew he wanted a real and deeper relationship with God. While other little boys played outside, he was at church in Bible study or prayer meetings or found himself helping to clean the church.

My husband shared about being bullied by classmates for his actions and his appearance. He was attacked physically by classmates, belittled, and made to feel like an outcast or a freak. The effects of bullying over extended periods of time can cause irreversible damage, especially on a child. My husband was timid. Irrespective of who the bully was, he remained silent about the abuse, and this silence was rooted in fear. He hid his emotions and carried the hurt, shame, and anger internally. He only felt a release in certain safe places, but not fully. To this day, he still harbors some negative thoughts and feelings concerning his childhood. He is working through his deliverance from the wounds of rejection, and I am praying for his complete healing in this area. I want him to feel and experience the power of freedom from everything that holds him captive.

My Layers

I had my own struggles. I admit that I too suffered from the curse of rejection. I experienced rejection from both my family and peers. Growing up with my "sister/cousins," I was different, and there were times when these sister/cousins would remind me of that. Sister/cousins are cousins who are more like sisters than cousins. You grow up together because you are close in age, and you cannot remember a childhood incident that did not include them. My mother had two sisters; both were married with children. My cousins would go home with their mom and dad while I stayed with my grandparents.

I loved being with my grandparents, and sometimes I would have a tantrum when my mother would come to pick me up. I believe my cousins were jealous of the relationship that I had with my grandparents. Probably because I was their favorite. Although that may have been true, my grandparents never displayed favoritism.

I recall being teased for being born the "natural way," and my cousins were born through C-section. Yes, that was a joke for many years. Children will find the most ridiculous things to joke about. My appearance was different—I was always the tallest and have dealt with facial acne my entire life. Children can be very mean and judgmental.

These are some of my scars that I suffered in silence for many years. Rejection was deepest and strongest when it came to my father. My father was not involved in my life the way a father should be. I knew my father and respected him in that role, but I was insecure. I did not understand why my father did not actively and permanently want to be involved in my life. This rejection created trust issues. I never wanted to get too close to anyone or develop long-lasting relationships. I didn't want to be tolerated or rejected by anyone. I would find myself not opening up to people, being distant. I knew I suffered hurt in this area and needed to be healed. I did not want to continue to harbor feelings of not being good enough or not fitting in because of my looks.

As a child, trying to fit in with others who ridiculed you and made you feel beneath them is awful. As a young adult developing and growing in God, I had to be honest about those insecurities and allow Him to heal me from the inside out. I had to go back to the Potter's wheel and be made over. When I allowed God to heal those hurts and insecurities, he revealed my true identity. I am the righteousness of God; I am fearfully and wonderfully made in His likeness and image. I am heir with God and joint heir with Christ, and I have the Greater (Christ) inside my heart! I had to forgive those who shamed me for whatever reason. I had to understand that my father's shortcomings were not mine. I am good and loved by my heavenly Father. Today, I admit I enjoy spending time alone and feel comfortable with myself. If there are things about myself I do not like, I change them.

Recently I buried my father, and God allowed me to give remarks about him. I had the opportunity to share my heart—my healed heart. And it was good.

Targeting the Layers

Feeling rejected is horrible. You feel like you do not fit, don't belong, or are simply not needed. As children, it is hard not knowing what to do with those feelings. Worst of all, it is hard not having someone you feel you can trust with your feelings. It is not good as an adult when you need help or someone to talk to but just *don't*. The devil does not like exposure. Satan will work overtime if he can stay hidden and keep you in the dark. Curses and negative strongholds attached to your life are damaging and unhealthy. Know and believe that God Himself wants you free.

I recently came across a blog written by Janine Rohrbaugh called "From His Presence." In it, there are four major areas that stand out in your life if rejection is the curse you struggle with:

1. Self-isolation
2. You think God rejected you
3. You keep things hidden from others to protect your heart
4. You are afraid of not being included

I am a child of the King of kings and the Creator of the world. God is my source and my strength. I seek Him concerning every area of my life. I pray fervently because my life depends on it. Prayer is my daily life secret. My walk with God, knowing and understanding who I am, and knowing my purpose, are essential to my existence. The following are a few scriptures that target rejection. There are others, but these will get you started on your journey of healing and deliverance:

- Psalms 94:14
- 2 Corinthians 12:9
- Isaiah 53:3
- John 1:11; 15:8
- Luke 10:16

Meditation

God did not bring us through the lies, warfare, tests, and trials for us to forfeit blessing.
You can't give up now—you're so close to the birthing of the blessings, miracles, coming outs, and coming throughs. Isaiah 66:9 says, "Shall I bring to the birth, and not cause to bring forth? saith the Lord: shall I cause to bring forth and shut the womb? saith thy God."

Chapter 2

FORGIVENESS

Meditation

> "For thou, Lord art good, and ready to forgive; and plenteous in mercy unto all of them that call upon thee" (Psalm 86:5). Forgive them for you. Often we're so consumed with what they did or said and fail to let go. We do not realize bitterness is growing. Refuse to allow unforgiveness to control or alter your life. Unforgiveness is a cancer.

How could I have allowed myself to end up here? He was built—I mean, he had muscles for days, he was tall, light skinned, and fine. He knew all the girls were checking him out too, this man so put together like a male body builder. His big, sexy chest and strong arms were calling my name, and the fact that his shirts were so tight did not help either. We saw him around school but did not know for sure which class he taught. You know how high school girls daydream about their male teachers, especially if they look good and are close to the same age. Well, that is what he had many of us doing. He was a full-grown man, not like the little high school boys. He had a good head of hair, and he was a little flirtatious. *Oh my goodness, here we go again!*

While sitting in church one day, I looked up, and guess who I saw walking in? Yes, Mr. Fine himself. Did he come looking for me? Or did he know someone here? Why was he here? As I continued to watch, I noticed there was a woman who walked in with him. *OK, so he was not looking for me.* They made their way to the middle of the church and sat pretty close to one another. I thought to myself, *She's cute, if that is his girlfriend.* They visited a couple more Sundays together and began to participate more in ministry. After a few weeks, they both became church members. I learned quickly that this woman was Mr. Fine's wife! I was shocked. Maybe they had not been married long because he sure did not act like he was married when he was at school. By this time I had graduated from high school, and he did not remember me.

Up until this point, I did not date guys at my church or bring anyone I was dating around church. The chance of dating someone at church and then breaking up with them was a horrible thought, and I did not want any church boys to know me like that.

I was nineteen when Mr. Fine started showing interest in me. Maybe he did remember me after all. I admit, during this time in my life I was dating carefree and having fun. I was making my own money and had a little taste of freedom. They were some good times, but they were some crazy times too. There were times I made a lot of foolish mistakes and wrong choices, choices that when I think back even today, I still regret. When he started showing interest in me, I should have known nothing good would come of it. I should have stuck with my own rule and not talked much with church guys, much less date them; that was my first mistake. It started out slow. We exchanged numbers and quickly started talking on the phone. That led to a little flirting at church, us showing up in the same locations, and working together on the same ministry projects. Two months in, we started to move things along in our phone conversations. We shifted from just checking in on each other and *what did I miss at church?* to *when can we meet for lunch?*

I have always felt more mature than boys my age, so talking to older men was never an issue for me. We eventually began to meet up. We started out doing the "church hug," and then that turned into a hug and a kiss on the cheek, and then a full make-out session. Then one day, we went way too far. I gave in to his advances, and I felt horrible. I was disgusted with myself. I could not believe how I ended up in bed with a married man. I replayed the conversations and encounters in my head. I hated myself for even allowing this to happen. I stopped taking his phone calls and even started dodging him at church. I was not mad at him as much as I was mad at myself and disappointed that I allowed this to happen. *How could I have done this?*

I stopped going to church as often. Praying was nothing I wanted to do. I felt like God really did not want to hear from me after what I had done. I resigned from leadership positions at church. This was very hard because, although I did not yet have a personal relationship with God, I still enjoyed working in ministry. I knew I needed to relinquish my duties, so I pulled away from most of my church friends. The mental torment was hell. I felt regret and remorse but did not know how to deal with those feelings and the torment. I also realized that I was probably not the only one he had been with, and that did not make it better. *How could I have been so gullible and foolish?*

How I was feeling on the inside eventually manifested on the outside. Weeks went by, and the hard knot down in the pit of my stomach was not yielding any relief. I knew then that I had to do something, but what? I repented the very night we slept together, but I knew I had to confess to God again and ask for forgiveness. One evening, I was listening to an evangelist share her testimony of learning how to forgive yourself. She said self-forgiveness is the hardest challenge you will ever face. Although this statement carries many levels, I found it to have such truth to it in this situation. I sat up in my bed and knew that was my problem—I was unable to forgive myself wholly and completely. I knew if I could get past the torment, I would feel better.

The next day, I reached out to an older spiritual mother to confide in. I was able to verbalize the incident to her without judgment or scorn. She prayed with me and shared some scriptures that I should read. I knew I was still carrying the guilt of unforgiveness. God had already forgiven me; I needed to forgive myself so I could be fully healed. Forgiving myself was a very self-reflecting, intense process. I learned that no matter what it is you need to forgive yourself for, whether big or small, the steps are the same. I needed to forgive myself because I knew better; he was married and a member of my church! But I did not want anyone from the church to find out about this. I knew I would be blamed for hurting their marriage. Thinking about it was bad enough. What we did affected not just us but his wife too. Disrespecting her and their marriage weighed heavily on me, and allowing this to happen was my biggest regret. The Bible declares in Mark 10:8, "And they twain shall be one flesh: so, then they are no more twain, but one flesh."

Prayer

Heavenly Father, we come to You in the name of Jesus our Savior. Lord, I lift this daughter up to You. Lord, You know the shame and hurt she is feeling. She repents of her sins and asks for forgiveness for the wrong she has done. Lord, You said that a broken spirit and contrite heart You would in no way despise. Father God, we ask that You blot out her transgressions and purge her with your hyssop. Create in her a clean heart, and renew within her a right spirit. Make her hear gladness like only You can. In Jesus' name, amen.

I may not have been the first or the last person this man slept with while being married, but I hated my role in the separation of their union. Some may not understand and think that the reason this happened in the first place was because their relationship was already rocky. That may be true, but the spiritual implications are on another level than just the physical. God ordained marriage before any other union. Marriage should not be entered into lightly. It should not be dishonored or taken for granted as just another relationship. God's desire for a marriage between a man and a woman is based on His relationship between Christ and His church. I was unsaved at the time I made this choice, but I knew it was not right. Spiritually, I had opened Pandora's box. I knew I needed to right the wrong, but how?

Eventually he and I had a conversation. I shared with him how I felt and assured him it would never happen again. It never did. Once I made that confession, I was able to start taking steps to forgive myself and heal. Ultimately, God is the only one who can heal every area of hurt. He must heal you so you can truly move forward in life.

Prayer

> *Father God, help me to forgive all those who have wronged me. Remove the spirit of unforgiveness in me that I may forgive and be forgiven. Root out the hurt and the pain, purge me, and wash me in Your blood. Stand strong in me and help me to cast my cares on You and*

> *to rest in Your love for me. Help me stand firm on Your word and think on the things that are true, that are honest, and that are just. Father, open my spiritual eyes and ears so that I may learn what I am to learn in this season and move as You would lead me. In Jesus' name, amen.*

1. *Receive forgiveness from God:* 1 John 1:9 states, "If we confess our sins, He is faithful and just to forgive us our sins and to cleanse us from all unrighteous." After repenting of the sin and praying about it, I picked up my Bible and tried to break the bubble I felt trapped in. I knew that God heard me when I prayed. I knew that God knew my heart, so now it was time for me to forgive myself.
2. *Acknowledge the mistake aloud:* James 5:16 asserts, "Confess your trespasses to one another, that you may be healed. The effective, fervent prayer of a righteous man avails much." Earlier, I shared how I spoke with a spiritual advisor. I did confess my transgression, and I felt a lot better. I felt a release. My encounters with her were ongoing. She understood my pain and saw my brokenness. She so willingly helped me through my process. She was a voice of reason and accountability. Whoever you may choose to help you walk through your process should be spiritually sound and able to cover you in prayer.

3. *Examine your mistakes:* Psalm 54:4 declares, "Against thee, thee only, have I sinned, and done evil in thy sight: that thou mightest be justified when thou justified when thou speakest, and be clear when thou judgest." I knew I needed to reflect on my actions and shortcomings and really think about *why* I chose to sin in this manner. It shouldn't have been so easy for me to fall into someone else's marriage bed. Even though I was not living a redeemed life, I still knew these things. James 4:17 says, "Therefore to him that knoweth to do good and doeth it not, to him it is sin." I knew I was living my so-called best life, but I knew this was unfamiliar, and I was moving into uncharted areas.

4. *Self-reflect and own your mistakes:* I recited the Serenity Prayer daily and quoted it around the clock. "God grant me the serenity to accept the things I cannot change, courage to change the things I can, and wisdom to know the difference." I messed up, but I won't let this one mistake stop me. In self-reflection, when I thought about being excited or glad that this man wanted to be intimate with me, I wondered what he really thought about me. What do I have attached to me that makes me so gullible and accessible to a married man? It was in this step that I had to take an in-depth look at myself and truly hear from God.

Meditation

> *Always see the treasure God has placed within you. Do not place too much value in the opinion of others. Trust that God knows what is in you, and He will choose you even when others overlook you.*

What Is Forgiveness?

Forgiveness is the deliberate willingness to let go of unwarranted feelings caused by oneself or other individual(s). *Psychology Today* says that forgiveness is "A willingness to drop the narrative on a particular injustice, to stop telling ourselves over and over again the story of what happened, what this other person did, how we were injured, and all the rest of the unforgivableness."[1] Forgiveness for me is freedom—freedom from the bondage of hurt, madness, sadness, betrayal, and fear. These words and the feelings associated with them, when carried around and held inside, are toxic. Going through the process of forgiving myself, I acknowledged that it was a self-inflicted wound. I did not consider my consequences. I learned also that when others cause you hurt, pain, and sadness, the wounds are felt internally. Irrespective of how the wounds impact us, they are unhealthy for the mind, body, and spirit. We

---

1. Suzanne Degges-White PhD. "Forgiveness Can Free You from the Past," *Psychology Today* (2021), https://www.psychologytoday.com/us/blog/lifetime-connections/202112/forgiveness-can-free-you-the-past.

must understand that to forgive is something the Lord is expecting us to do.

I realized that I was wrestling within myself and not forgiving myself and not willing to accept that God had forgiven me. God forgave me the first time I asked, and that was hard to embrace. But eventually I did embrace it. Our Lord is gracious and forgiving, looking beyond our faults and seeing us and our every need. As the Lord's Prayer says, "Forgive us our debts, as we forgive our debtors." The Bible provides many scriptures that state that when we can forgive others, we will be blessed! When you can give God your hurt, pain, and wounded spirit caused by another person, and feel the release of casting that care over to Him, you are blessed. You are an overcomer; you are a winner in Christ.

For me, it truly is a *woosah* moment! In my *woosah* (a feeling of calm and relaxation) moments, I feel the presence of God so close and so real, like He is literally holding me in His arms and rocking me, wiping my tears away. He lifts me above the hurt and gives me clarity and peace in my inner being and freedom from the weight that is indescribable. I pray that everyone who reads my story will experience this awesome feeling of knowing that the Lord Himself is in every situation that concerns you and will fight with you and for you.

I Was Forgiven, So I Must Forgive

I admit, when I first found out about my husband's infidelity, the pain I felt was like someone had taken a dagger to my heart and carved out all of my insides, threw them into the trash to be broken, and smashed some more. For me to breathe was hard and distressing—with every breath I took, my strength would leave. I was shattered! And I felt every broken piece. My hurt and pain were deep. I never imagined I would feel pain like this.

My thoughts immediately went to my own transgressions. I hated to think that I was the cause of this pain. The devil started bringing all kinds of thoughts to my mind. He wanted me to carry the weight of my past and blame me for my present marital state. I began to think that I was reaping what I had sowed, that I was getting back what I gave out. Satan wanted me to feel ugly, worthless, and unloved. It appeared that all of a sudden, every weapon the devil had was formed to destroy me.

Days turned into months and months into years, and the pain was still fresh with every new day. I was just existing, doing the bare minimum. Looking beyond the moment was not a thought. I remember going to the Word because I needed clarity and direction. My husband and the devil were trying to get me to believe that this was all my fault. Galatians 6:7-8a says, "Be not deceived; God is not mocked: for whatsoever a man soweth that shall he also reap. For he that soweth to his flesh shall of the flesh reap corruption." The chapter before this is Paul talking to the Galatians and encouraging them to stand firm in their faith. I admit, I was losing faith. But thanks be unto God who always causes us to triumph! When it seemed like the stop clock was counting me out and that I was forfeiting the game, after reading the Word of God I chose to not stay down. Instead, I looked to God—the Author and Finisher of my faith—to shelter me through my difficult marriage. I took God at His Word, I stood on His Word, and I trusted His Word, and today, with the strength of God, I walk in His Word. "But the God of all grace, who hath called us unto his eternal glory by Christ Jesus, after that ye have suffered awhile, make you perfect, stablish, strengthen, settle you" (1 Peter 5:10).

I knew I needed to forgive my husband. Does that mean I would forget? By no means. God is not constantly thinking about our past sins, as we do when we allow our flesh to control us. We read in the book of Matthew, "Then Peter came up and said to Him, Lord, how often shall my brother sin against me, and I forgive him? As many as seven times? Jesus said to him, 'I do not say to you seven times, but seventy times seven'" (Matthew 18:210-22). There are times when you may think about the offense, but that is not a place where you should dwell or visit often because ill feelings will manifest. There are times when I may want to say something and throw things up in his face, but I choose not to—and it's not that I haven't forgiven him, but it is me being human. There are times when I check my spirit to make sure I'm not in my flesh or angry when we do begin to discuss painful past issues. Proper communication is key to any successful relationship.

When we began to talk about the past, I wanted to explore his thoughts and feelings as to why there was a crack in our foundation. We both needed to be honest with our feelings because if we couldn't be real with ourselves and God, we couldn't be real with anyone. Even after acknowledging our feelings and after I forgave my husband, there were still times when I hoped he would reap the consequences from his actions. I wanted him to understand the severity of his actions and turn from his fleshly ways, but I didn't desire to brow beat him or attack him about it. I know that the Lord sees and is aware of our every action and thought; He sits high but looks low. Romans 12:19 says, "Vengeance is mine, I will repay, says the Lord." I have to know that as I stand on and rest in God, He's got me. He is mindful of every area of my life.

With God, all things are possible. As I write my story, it has definitely opened up a lot of past emotions and feelings that I knew at times wouldn't be easy, but I have been determined and intentional to share. I chose to forgive and walk in forgiveness, but I have seen my share of people who don't want to forgive and let go of hurt and offenses. I have seen the shell of someone staying in a difficult marriage who, with every word and action, their bitterness and anger grows. I have a good friend who often shares her wisdom moments with me. It's during these times that the Lord reveals His heart to her. As I read and meditate on what God is saying through my friend, it changes my heart.

I'm able to walk in forgiveness and open up today because of the change that took place even before my marriage. My time of shattering was not a walk in the park—I was bruised, and others saw my bruises. I was ridiculed and gossiped about by close associates, and I was made to feel unloved and unworthy. The best way to describe me walking in forgiveness is to compare it to a metamorphosis. I like to think that if you saw me today, you would see the biggest, brightest butterfly in flight. According to Webster's Dictionary, *metamorphosis* is a change of the form or nature of a thing or person into a completely different one, by natural or supernatural means. My change was no doubt a supernatural one. It was no one but my Lord who changed me from the inside. A butterfly goes through four stages before it is birthed into what we see flying around. Just as you look at the end result of a butterfly and see the vivid and extravagant colors, you couldn't imagine the process it had to go through to get to look that way. The metamorphosis of a butterfly's process is a radical one. The dramatic change in every step must not be taken lightly or disturbed, for it will cause the entire process to be terminated.

  The first stage of the metamorphosis is called the egg stage. In the egg stage, the female butterfly must choose the right plant to lay (hatch) their eggs on. This is crucial in the process because this plant is where the caterpillar will get its nourishment to survive. In my recollection of fifth-grade science, in butterfly metamorphosis, the caterpillar is wrapped up and hidden for weeks before developing into a butterfly. The noticeable changes and growth make this transformation that much more fascinating. It's there in the cocoon that the caterpillar is shaped and made new. The caterpillar as we know it no longer exists; it now has wings, eyes, and organs to reproduce. The hardness of the cocoon is there to protect the process so that no nourishment is lacking. At the end of the metamorphosis, you see no signs that this was ever a caterpillar—everything is new. A new look, a new way of existing, and a new way of moving in the world.

Prayer

> *Dear God, today I ask You to help me forgive my husband. I acknowledge that I have allowed his actions and words to cause me to harbor wrong thoughts and feelings. Teach me how to forgive and let go of the feelings of desiring to get even. Lord, teach me and help me to forgive even if he is selfish and not sorry for his actions. Today I ask You to mend my heart and guard my mind and thoughts. I release it today. In Jesus' name, amen.*

When I initially learned of my husband's betrayal, I wanted to crawl up into my cocoon and die. I wanted to be hidden from the shame and embarrassment, but I had to remember that I chose the Lord to be the head of my life. So I had to trust His will and direction for what was best for my life. As I began to ask the questions, *Why me? Why us?*, I remembered that Jesus is the True Vine. John 15:5 (NLT) says, "Yes, I am the vine, you are the branches. Those who remain in me, and I in them, will produce much fruit. For apart from me you can do nothing." Before I said yes to my husband, I had chosen a sure foundation, the True Vine. As I remembered that, I was able to find rest.

The larva is the second stage. In this stage, the caterpillar begins to eat and grow. The growth is rapid and vital. During this stage, the caterpillar is delicate, and the right amount of time must be given to ensure proper maturation. In my larva stage, I was very sensitive to the Spirit of God. During this time, I would fast from food and other forms of entertainment. I didn't completely understand, but there was an urgency in my spirit, and I had to obey. I was told that when you fast, you deny yourself (your flesh) of your sin nature's wants and desires. It's in this time of longing where you direct your attention more acutely to hearing from God. Isn't it funny that when we, the body of Christ, fast from physical nourishment, that's when we grow and gain strength to endure? In my larva stage, I put on strength by obeying the voice of the Lord. I went to church daily by myself to pray at the altar. I didn't really pray outwardly, but on the inside I called on God with every ounce of strength. Slowly but surely, I could feel my help and my strength increase.

    I wept and listened. I felt like Hannah in the book of 1 Samuel as I went into prayer. Hannah experienced pain, hurt, and shame, but she knew if she could just get to the temple and get in the presence of God, things would be better. There were days when I don't know how I drove myself to church. My mind was cloudy, but once I made it into the church, the presence of God overwhelmed me, and I ran to the altar. One day while lying there, I heard a *rhema* word. *Christianity Today* defines a rhema word as "an inspired word birthed within your own spirit, a whisper from the Holy Spirit like the still, small voice."[2] Just like that, I heard, *I am a present help*. I got up, wiped my tears, fixed myself up, and walked out of the church. I felt a renewed sense of self. I felt purpose. I felt like a

---

    2. Hope Bolinger, "What is the Rhema Word," *Christianity Today* (March 20, 2020), https://www.christianity.com/wiki/bible/what-is-the-rhema-word.html.

new creation. I cherish the very presence of God—to go through such betrayal and feel like an outcast and then to be lifted and liberated by God is incredible. In my season of fasting and praying while resting in the True Vine, I received my nourishment!

The third stage is when the caterpillar slowly turns into the pupa, which is the beginning of the butterfly. The shell of the chrysalis is initially soft, but it becomes hard in order to protect the body of the butterfly. In my pupa stage, I began to open up and share my testimony with others. I shared intimate details with my mentors, something I was not able to do before. Sure, they were aware of my state of affairs, but it wasn't until I began to allow my Protector to protect me when I felt comfortable in my own skin and could talk. I started to share my testimony with other young ladies who were in difficult marriages or who had experienced the same or similar events in their lives but didn't know how to get past the hurt. I opened up and started to put words with my feelings. I had some clarity, where I once was confused as to who I saw in the mirror. Though this mirror was cracked, I could see enough. I could see the bruises and the shame, but I also saw my husband being transformed. I saw what God was saying. I became more conscious and self-aware of what was actually taking place.

In the fourth and final stage, the butterfly appears. The fluid, the nectar, is important because it is needed to guarantee that the butterfly has all it needs to emerge and soar. In my last stage where I transformed into a butterfly, I broke out of my cocoon, knowing and feeling as if I could do all things through Christ who strengthens me! I knew just as in every other stage that the Lord was right there with me, waiting to anoint me with fresh oil. His fresh oil symbolizes the Spirit of God, assuring me that He is with me and preparing me for greater things.

    Today as I look back, I can appreciate the process. I can appreciate the fact that God is mindful of me. *I was forgiven, and I walk in forgiveness.*

Chapter 3

THE SHATTERED WIFE

Meditation

For I know the plans that I have for you, my daughter. Continue to be faithful in doing well. You are kept for my glory. I will bring you forth to display my glory. You are being refined. I, God, am doing a work. It is not a man. It is my glory revealed in the earth; I keep you for my glory. "For it is my will and it pleases me," says the Lord. Harden not your heart at those who have made your way hard. I have allowed it for my glory to come to pass in you, daughter. For you are chosen to bring my glory. "I speak well of you; I speak well of you," says the Lord.

Some may say, *I was already shattered before I became a wife.* I would agree before I accepted the Lord. I was shattered, but when I said, "I do," the Lord made me whole. First Thessalonians 5:23-24 says, "Now may the God of peace make you holy in every way, and may your whole spirit and soul and body be kept blameless until our Lord Jesus Christ comes again. God will make this happen, for He who calls is faithful."

To *shatter* is to break at once into pieces and to damage badly. Admittedly, I lost myself once I got married. I still loved the Lord and was committed to Him, yet I allowed my circumstances and surroundings to dictate my emotions. I became overwhelmed with new changes in my life—I was a new wife, and I don't know about you, but I wasn't given a handbook. I was thrown into a new lifestyle, I became part of a new family, and I had a new level of demons creeping around. I moved and performed in my own strength. It took me a minute, but soon I learned that you can never achieve much and remain whole without the strength and help of God.

I was born in the early 70s, a time when many things in the world were changing: politics, hairstyles, music, and fashion. My mother once shared with me that she wanted a baby because she wanted her very own doll like her two older sisters. Growing up, I spent most of my years living in my grandparents' home. I was raised by my grandmother and trained by my mother, and in much of my foundation I was taught to treat others the way I would want to be treated, to respect everyone, and to never look down on anyone. We weren't wealthy, but we had what we needed.

I was taken to church as a child and learned the importance of who God is as well as the inner workings of ministry. I recall spending time with my sanctified great aunt on my grandmother's side at church. We called her Aunt Mandie. She would call to speak to my grandmother but would often end up talking to me. Aunt Mandie was a prayer warrior, and I believe that while she was giving me candy and talking to me, she was praying for me too. I believe she was praying for my future as well as for my health and protection. I believe she prayed on that day that I would have my own personal relationship with Christ and that the Lord would keep a hedge of protection around me. I remember when she passed away—I was five years old. Her death caused a dramatic shattering in our family dynamic. She was a leader in our family and in the church. It is because of her relationship with God that my grandmother's household was introduced to Christ and was reared in the Pentecostal Reformation. I am forever grateful for her life and prayers, knowing that the seeds she sowed into my life are still being watered today. Because of her, I'm here by the grace of God. Today, I smile and thank God for a spirit of prayer, knowing that Aunt Mandie's prayers and faith have contributed to the woman, wife, and mother I am. I have experienced several shattering incidents in my life that could have been left broken, *but God!*

On one occasion as a child, I was told to lie still on the bed as we traveled down the long, cold corridors of the hospital where my mother worked as a nurse. I was very familiar with most of the areas, especially the playroom and the cafeteria. On this particular visit, though, things were different. My mother wasn't wearing her uniform, and we didn't go to her floor. Eventually while on the elevator, I heard someone say we were headed to the basement. It was even colder down there. As we entered the room, there was a smaller bed, a chair, and a big machine. I got off the big bed I was on and switched to the smaller bed. I was clueless as to what would happen next. I liked going to work with my mother, so I was excited just to be there. As I laid on the bed, I remember someone putting something white and sticky in my hair. Then they added yellow and green wires to the sticky things. It didn't hurt, and I wasn't even scared at this point because my mom was with me the whole time, holding my hand.

After all the wires were stuck to my head, they began to hook the wires to the machine. Once it turned on, it showed many pictures and lines moving. Not a word was said. I guess they figured my mother had told me why I was there and what would take place. But how do you explain this to your four-year-old doll? I stayed still in the same position for hours and eventually fell asleep. I believe once I fell asleep, my mother left the room. Just like that, when I woke up, it was time to leave. As a young child, I returned to the hospital every so often for that same procedure. It was later on in my life when I learned that I had epilepsy.

According to the Epilepsy Foundation, "epilepsy is a brain disorder that causes recurring, unprovoked seizures."[3] When I was about three years old, I fell from a two-story apartment complex. By the grace of God,

---

3. Epilepsy Foundation, "What is Epilepsy?" (2023), https://www.epilepsy.com/what-is-epilepsy.

I had no breaks, tears, or scaring. But I was told I had really bad seizures. With seizures, once the seizure is over you really don't remember what happened. I'm not sure if my mother was ever told the reason behind the seizures. I learned that the procedures I was having were called EEGs, and they were to check my brain activity and to learn more about my seizures. They wanted to know what was causing them. During this time many years ago, there was a negative stigma attached to people with seizures—people thought you were strange or weird. Some thought they meant you were demon possessed or that you had mental issues. I don't know exactly when they started for me or when they ended, but eventually I grew out of them.

There's a story in the book of Mark where Jesus heals a boy with an unclean spirit. Often, I speak of this miracle healing when I testify of my own healing. Mark 9:20-27 says,

> And they brought him unto him: and when he saw him, straightway the spirit tare him; and he fell on the ground, and wallowed foaming. And he asked his father, How long is it ago since this came unto him? And he said, Of a child. And ofttimes it hath cast him into the fire, and into the waters, to destroy him: but if thou canst do any thing, have compassion on us, and help us. Jesus said unto him, "if thou canst believe, all things are possible to him that believeth." And straightway the father and the child cried out, and said with tears, Lord I believe; help thou my unbelief.

> When Jesus saw that the people came running together, He rebuked the foul spirit, saying unto him, "Thou dumb and deaf spirit, I charge thee, come out of him, and enter no more into him." And the spirit cried, and rent him sore, and came out of him: and he was as one dead; insomuch that many said he is dead. But Jesus took him by the hand and lifted him up; and he arose.

It is a blessing when you can pray for your own healing, but sometimes your faith may not be strong enough, and someone else may need to step in and intercede for you. This is called an intercessory prayer, and the person praying and seeking God on someone else's behalf is called an intercessor. Aunt Mandie was my intercessor. Thank you, Aunt Mandie, for laying hands on me and praying for healing for me. *Thank You, God, for hearing her prayers and healing my mind, body, and spirit.* The famous Dr. Seuss says, "When something bad happens you have three choices. You can either let it define you, let it destroy you, or you can let it strengthen you."

As I write, I'm reminded of the scripture that says, "The thief cometh not, but for to steal, and to kill, and to destroy: I am come that they might have life, and that they might have it more abundantly." You can guess which life I chose. Yes, I chose an abundant life! I will never forget the day I walked into the prayer meeting determined not to leave the same—not to leave without receiving the greatest gift anyone can receive. On June 3, 1995, during the noon day prayer, I received the Holy

Spirit into my life at the age of twenty-one. I craved the indwelling and fullness of the Holy Spirit.

Growing up charismatic, our leaders and elders taught, testified, and preached about the Holy Spirit—that you can't feel whole or complete without Him. Before I committed my life to Christ and received the gift of the Holy Spirit, I knew I needed to make changes in my life. I felt stuck and unfulfilled. I wanted the blessings of the Lord but didn't want to give Him control of my life. During this time, a very horrific incident took place in my life that sent me spiraling into darkness. It could have left me shattered, but I chose not to let it define me.

One night during Christmas break, my friends and I went to a popular night spot where the young, mature crowd would hang out. While there, I locked eyes with someone I had met there a few weeks ago, and he made his way over to me. He was there with friends as well. We talked for a while, and soon he started to get a little frisky with his hands. I kind of liked him and the attention, so I didn't mind him touching me a little. But I could tell he was getting more and more intoxicated. I remember the Bobby Brown song "Roni" was playing. He became more and more aggressive and eventually asked if I wanted to leave with him. I said, *No!* I didn't want to leave yet, and I was uncomfortable leaving with him, knowing he had been drinking.

I could tell he was upset when he walked away from me. He walked outside and then came back in and walked right back toward me. He came up behind me very closely and whispered in my ear, "Get your $#*% and let's go!" He then pressed something really hard into my back. At first, I couldn't tell what it was, but then I realized it was the barrel of a gun. He told me not to make any sudden moves, all while slowly rocking me back and forth as if we were dancing. I was petrified, thinking, *This dude is crazy! Who have I gotten myself involved with?* I didn't know what to do—all I could feel was the gun pressing hard against me, bruising my skin. I slowly grabbed my things and told my friends I was going to leave with him. They were shocked and thought I was crazy, and I could tell they were a little disappointed I was leaving.

We made it out to his car, and I started to plead with him not to do this. It was pointless. He pulled the gun out so I could see it as he directed me into the car. He then took my phone and started driving. He stopped at a neighborhood store, and as he walked in, some of my classmates pulled up in a car next to me. It was dark, so I wasn't sure if anyone could recognize me let alone see me. I wanted to yell and scream to get their attention, but I was afraid of what he might do if I got caught. I knew that that would probably be my last chance to get away too.

He got back in the car and we drove away. The whole time he didn't say a word to me. Eventually we pulled up to an old, dark house—it looked like no one was home. He pulled me out of the car, pointing his gun straight at me while he whispered, "Be quiet." He didn't want to wake his grandmother. He led me straight back to his room and proceeded to sexually assault me. I thank God that the assault did not last long. I called on Jesus, praying that I wouldn't lose my life or be left with any physical scars from this. Afterward, he let me go.

I got home just before dawn the next morning. I was hurt and ashamed. Initially I blamed myself—I felt dumb that I allowed myself to be put into a situation where I could have lost my life. *But God.* It took about a week for me to share what happened with my mother because I was embarrassed. My body still hurt, and I was in pain emotionally, mentally, and every way in between. The more I tried to forget and let go of that night, the worse things got. I went to the doctor to make sure it was nothing more serious physically and was given medication to alleviate the physical pain. But the emotional pain still lingered. I knew I needed to face the incident head on and process every detail of what had happened and stop pretending it was just a bad dream. I didn't want to face the fact that I was a statistic and needed to talk to someone.

    I did end up going to a therapist to talk. It felt good to open up and verbalize what happened and hear the therapist's point of view. It took me several meetings with the therapist before I felt able to turn and talk to God about what happened to me. On one particular Sunday, after I heard a powerful message from my pastor, I knelt at the altar and thanked and praised God for allowing me to make it through the ugliness. I pleaded with God for the ability to finally let it go. After that day, I stopped going out late with friends, and I never shared what happened to me that night with anyone else.

    God stepped in during that moment in my life. He held me by the hand and healed me from the grotesque feelings, the hurt, and the shame of that night. Up until that point, the devil tried to get me to believe that because I was violated and broken emotionally and because I had suffered in silence, that I was useless. But the truth is that many in the Bible have powerful testimonies of healing and deliverance, and God used them *because of* their shattered past, not *in spite of*. Consider people like Job, Hannah, and Esther. They endured deeply shattering events in their lives, but they also experienced the sheltering of God. I learned during my shattered times that when I felt the most broken and wounded, that was when I demonstrated the most humility. I was humbled to obey the voice of God and to hear Him when He said in a faint voice, *You still have purpose.*

As long as there is breath in our bodies, our lives still have meaning. If you are involved in a dangerous accident of some kind, the first responder will check your pulse. *There's still hope.* This hope is what God means when He says to call on Him in our time of need. No matter what has happened in our lives, He will answer! God will allow us to be shattered at times in order to get our attention. Psalm 34:18-20 declares, "The Lord is nigh unto them that are of a broken heart; and saveth such as be of a contrite spirit. Many are the afflictions of the righteous: But the Lord delivereth him out of them all. He keepeth all his bones: not one of them is broken." When I tell you I gave my life to God on June 3, 1995, I truly did. I allowed my heavenly Father access to every area of my life. I was tired of existing and daily trying to please and appease others.

Things changed for me after I gave my life and my past to God, and doors began to open as I walked with Him. I let go of the hurt and the damage that kept me bound and weighed down. I let go of the thoughts of, *I'm not good enough. I'm not a good daughter. I'm not as good as my cousins. I don't fit in. I'm always overlooked by my peers.* I stopped bearing the weight of familial curses and dysfunction that were attached to me from family matters, traumas, and bad choices I made. I grew in my knowledge of God, focused and obedient to His Word. I involved myself in church and enjoyed my new walk and commitment to Christ. It felt good to know I was chosen by God, that I could still be used by God, and that He has a plan for my life. *I'm a chosen vessel!*

I was married in the fall of 1990. My wedding day was beautiful and warm. The ceremony was at 6 p.m., and I remember leaving the house early that morning to take care of some last-minute details. I was nervous and excited. I couldn't believe I was getting M-A-R-R-I-E-D! I never dreamed I would one day marry and have a family and children of my own. I was in a good place spiritually and emotionally. I had prayed, and I believe the Lord gave His approval for my marriage. That evening, family members, church family, friends, and even my husband's ex was in attendance (I was told she was "just a friend"). I was ready for married life.

My husband really enjoyed cooking and preparing new dishes. He would cook, and I would clean. I thought everything in our lives would be good as long as we kept the Lord first and respected each other. I tried not to be a nagging or needy wife. I gave him space in the beginning to continue his routine. I allowed him space and time to prepare for his sermons because he was a man of God. I helped him prepare for church services, and I even ironed his handkerchiefs. I made sure the home was quiet as he studied the Bible. I desired to be a good help meet: "And the Lord said, it is not good that man should be alone; I will make him a help meet for him" (Genesis 2:18). There are plenty of books on marriage, but there is no handbook on how to be married to my particular husband.

It is important for wives to understand what the scriptures say about husbands and wives. The woman was made for the man to be his helper. Sometimes men don't allow their wives to help them. Shame on that man for forfeiting his opportunity to have a marriage, life, and family as God fully intended. God wanted both the man and the woman to coexist together as he leads and she helps him fulfill his accomplishments on Earth and they grow in spiritual union. In the beginning of our marriage, I didn't quite understand the scriptures myself, and my husband didn't either. I tried to do and be everything for my husband, and I lost my identity in the process. I tried tirelessly to emulate the Proverbs 31 woman—the virtuous woman. *Virtuous* simply means having or showing high moral standards. In the many women's study groups I participated in, they told us "the virtuous woman" is who you emulate, especially if you are married. I heard testimonies of married women and thought, *Oh my . . . I can be a virtuous woman if I work hard at pleasing my husband and do everything he wants me to do.* I was committed to satisfying his every need, and what I couldn't do I tried to learn. I wanted to be his missing rib; I wanted to please my husband and work hard to have a blessed marriage and home. According to Proverbs 31:10, "Who can find a virtuous woman? For her price is far above rubies." That's me! "The heart of her husband doth safely trust in her," Proverbs 31:11 says. I thought, *I know he trusts me. I'm a good church girl. I would never do anything to embarrass or hurt him.*

When I got married, I left my mother's house and moved in with my husband. I wasn't used to working to help with the household finances, but I was willing to work if that pleased him. If I had a job, he would be the primary breadwinner. I was fine with him managing the household budget. I knew I would have to sacrifice a lot, but that's part of being married. We are to consider each other's needs above our own.

I smiled when I read Proverbs 31:23: "Her husband is known in the gates, when he sitteth among the elders of the land." Because my husband was a well-known preacher in his hometown, his reputation warranted me diving deeper into the Word so that when I opened my mouth, I wouldn't sound foolish. I learned early that I was under a spotlight from what I wore to how I talked. Though I never desired to be a preacher's wife, I took my role as such very seriously. I wanted to be a godly example for my husband, my peers, and other young women I encountered.

I knew I had the favor of God with me. *Favor* is God's grace that He gives so that we can accomplish anything according to His will. The Bible also says, "Whoso findeth a wife findeth a good thing, and obtaineth favor from the Lord" (Proverbs 18:22). I must tell you, however, that I did not start out walking in the favor of God, nor did I understand just how much of his (my husband's) favor I was. I didn't completely understand the dynamics of marriage and how the husband is commanded to love his wife as Christ loved the church and gave his life for it. I feared the Lord. I was fine just being my husband's wife. I knew he was very outgoing and loved attention, and I was content to stand in his shadow.

My husband was a smooth talker, and he enjoyed the attention of women. On one occasion during our engagement, we went to a local store to register for wedding gifts. The store clerk was close to our parents' age, but that didn't stop her from flirtatiously smiling the entire time she helped us. And he smiled right back. Like most engaged women, I felt and hoped things like that would stop once we were married. Surely he wouldn't need to have that much attention, or surely his need to get and give every woman in the room attention would cease then. I quickly learned that as for me and my house, that was not so.

I was shattered early in my marriage. My thoughts and hopes for my marriage were interrupted like a massive freight train running through a small town—loud and shaking up and breaking everything in its path. I was hit hard. Everything I was doing to honor my husband and try to make him happy—by making our house a home and ensuring I never disrespected him, especially with the attention of another man—was not valued or appreciated. I saw my marriage shatter into many pieces. And every piece of glass had something written on it: *generational curse, idolatry, adultery, infidelity, lies, betrayal, hurt, etc.* I was no longer the girl behind the glass, living a fairy-tale story. I was the shattered wife in a drama series.

I will never forget the day my husband confessed his betrayal to me—that is, an affair that nearly ended our marriage. When he first confessed, I was numb. I didn't know what to say or do. I got my things and left. I'm an analyzer; I can sit and ponder things for hours or days before I speak, and this was definitely one of those times. I can dissect the smallest action or statement made by an individual. It took me some time before I could say anything in response to this life-changing news. This stabbing, gut-wrenching pain had created so many emotions and thoughts that were racing through my head. The only thing that kept me semi sane at that moment was my children. The thought of flipping out or "catching a case" and showing up on primetime news didn't happen because of my daughters. My very existence was fading; life as I knew it could not remain the same.

As a mother, my first thought is usually my children. How do I protect and shield them from this? My first priority was to protect my children. I tried not to show or express the hurt in front of them. I tried not to let them hear me weeping and crying out. I tried the best I could to save face for them. I didn't want them to know of my pain. I didn't want them to be mad at their father or hate him for the choices he had made. But the craziest thing was not only did I want to shield my children, but I also found myself protecting my husband. There were times I didn't go to certain church services or family functions to protect my family. I never demeaned my husband to my children; I never spoke an unkind word to them about anything their father had done. I know the respect that my daughters have today for their father is because of the restraint I possessed, and I give all glory to God.

As a wife, I wanted out! I wanted to leave the very day he confessed. I wanted to hurt him and cause him pain just like he caused me. I wanted to broadcast his betrayal to family and friends. I wanted him to be fired as a pastor! I didn't care about supporting him anymore or pretending for his reputation. I didn't care about his reputation or his ministry. I tried many times to warn my husband about things and people he was associating with within the church as well as outside the church. I wanted to get revenge and cause his world to shatter as he had done mine. As a pastor's wife, I wanted to *never* walk back into that church again.

I was amazed at the depth of maliciousness that goes on in church—how people can plot against each other. Countless times I wanted to confront the very ones who assisted in orchestrating this entanglement and let them know I see them. For many days and years I sat and suffered in silence, seeing the grins, smirks, and even tears for me. I know I was the topic of many of the church members' family discussions. The church building was never the same for me after that. But I have forgiven those who participated and celebrated this calamity. I have prayed for the many souls, young and old, who had to endure this disgusting stain that marred our church walls.

Chapter 4

THE MAN OF GOD

Prayer

Father God, in the name of Jesus, Lord, I thank You for this man, my husband, your man of God. Father, You made him, You called him, and You know all about him. I pray, oh God, that You would order his steps. I pray, dear God, that You would direct his path and give him the desire to wholly trust in You. I pray that Your will for his life will always be done. In Jesus' name, amen.

God's Word Concerning the Matter

The Spirit of the Lord is upon me, because he hath anointed me to preach the gospel to the poor; he hath sent me to heal the brokenhearted, to preach deliverance to the captives, and recovering sight to the blind, to set at liberty them that are bruised, to preach the acceptable year of the Lord. (Luke 4:18-19)

My husband, the man of God, the noted Reverend Titus Christopher Lawrence, was born and raised in a small rural town. He was raised by both his parents along with the strict teachings of his paternal and maternal grandparents. As a young boy he was shy, quiet, and mild-mannered. He accepted his call into ministry early in his life. As a child, Titus Christopher spent a lot of time by himself, listening for the voice of God, preaching to himself, and receiving wisdom from older men and women. Growing up in the country, he was shown the value of hard work as he watched his father provide for his family. Titus Christopher learned early that it is primarily the man's role to provide for his family and home. Though he never minded working with his hands, nor has he ever been ashamed of where he is from, he knew one day he would leave that small town. I think he has always been a big dreamer and knew that the Lord heard his prayers. He was and is a person of great faith.

After graduating from high school, my husband went off to college a couple hours from his hometown. He was excited to get the opportunity to attend college because he knew it would open many doors for him. Being away at school is a time when most young people, away from home for the very first time, look for the best parties and night spots. Instead, Titus Christopher tried to get to the local church and meet the pastor. He conducted church services on campus and encouraged many of his peers to join the religious clubs at school. My husband knew the church, church culture, and the Bible! I don't know what he would do if he couldn't preach and teach the Word of God. Through it all, I do believe he is walking in his God-given purpose.

I have always thought my husband was a good man. Before we were married, I remember praying for him and his ministry. I used to journal, and a few of my entries were about him. I knew then that my feelings for him were like nothing I had ever felt for anyone, but I never shared these feelings with him. I was so excited when I got to spend a few hours with him. I only wanted what was best for him. The more we spent time together, the more acquainted we got with one another. He never mentioned other girls, but I felt like he was spending his time with someone else. I eventually found out from a friend that he was engaged to be married. *Goodness!*

After finding out this news, I got a call from him. I said, "Congratulations." He responded, "For what?" He had no clue what I was talking about. I said, "Your engagement." You could have bought him for a penny, he was surprised I knew about it. Was I hurt? I was more disappointed than hurt. My disappointment was because we had just spent time together for my birthday, and at that time, as crazy as it sounds, I was kind of hoping for a marriage proposal.

I immediately cut ties with him. That was painful. I didn't think it would hurt as much as it did. I cried for a couple of days. I didn't want to lose a good friend, but I knew I needed to cut off communication. For a while after that, I sincerely prayed for him and his ministry.

My prayers for him were unselfish. My prayers for him were true and pure. I prayed that the will of the Lord would be done in his life. Though I loved him, I didn't fight for him or reveal my feelings to him.

Exactly one year later, we happened to run into one another at a church service. We were both pleasantly surprised to see each other, but of course, I couldn't let it be too obvious. Besides, I was there with my date, and I was certain his wife was nearby. We spoke politely, and as I gazed into his brown eyes and he grabbed my hand, the chemistry was palpable. I felt my heart skip a beat and my hands begin to tingle. I found out later from a friend that he felt the chemistry too. I didn't have time to ask any questions. I wanted to know how he was doing and how married life was treating him, but our encounter was brief since we were leaving the service. As we parted ways, my date opened the car door for me, and we drove off. I could still see Titus Christopher standing there in the mirror. I can't explain it, but I knew he would call me. And sure enough, I was awakened the next morning to Reverend Titus Christopher's voice on my phone. He started talking like nothing had happened. I said, "Excuse me, how is married life treating you?" Complete, dead silence. Then he blurted out, "I decided not to marry her." I responded, "Oh, you didn't marry her?" I was both nervous and happy, and inside I was dancing.

I couldn't wait to hear his explanation for why he broke off his engagement. I thought to myself, *This is going to be interesting.* Everyone was excited and talking about this wedding. Everyone knew it would be one of the most lavish weddings ever. Why? Because he was a well-known evangelist, and she was a member of a prominent out-of-state ministry. But I need to be honest—I really didn't care why he didn't marry her; I was just glad he didn't. He shared how they wanted to go in different directions in life—he wanted to advance in ministry, and she wanted to advance in her career. I didn't really know the woman, and I never asked him too many questions about her, but I can imagine that she was committed to her career and was not willing to compromise. Although I was glad the wedding had been called off, I kind of felt a little sad for him. He was in his late twenties and not getting younger. He wanted to advance his ministerial career, and he knew he needed a wife.

I must admit, I was jealous when I first heard about the engagement. Just knowing he would marry someone else was not a good feeling for me. But now, circumstances had changed. I could possibly have a chance at being Mrs. Titus Christopher Lawrence, and that sounded kind of nice to me. I was thinking, *Truly this is the Lord's doing, and it is marvelous in my eyes!* By this time, and as I had become more mature in God, my thoughts were, *I love the Lord and would love the opportunity to serve in ministry with this man.* I knew I would look good on his arm. After much prayer and fasting, I eventually ended my relationship with the other guy I was dating. Eventually Reverend Titus Christopher asked me to marry him, and our story as husband and wife is still being written. Today, we have been married well over thirty years.

The Bible describes the man of God in 1 Timothy 3:1-7:

> This is a true saying, if a man desires the office of bishop, he desireth a good work. A bishop then must be blameless, the husband

> of one wife, vigilant, sober, of good behavior, given to hospitality, apt to teach; not given to wine, no striker, not greedy of filthy lucre; but patient, not a brawler, not covetous; one that ruleth his own house, having his children in subjection with all gravity; for if a man know not how to rule his own house, how shall he take care of the church of God? Not a novice, lest being lifted up with pride he fell into the condemnation of the devil.

In the scriptures, Paul suggests that the desire to be a leader in the church is a good thing, but it requires you to possess certain godly characteristics such as being pleasing in the sight of God and blameless before man. Paul explains how men of God, leaders in the church, should conduct themselves. The Apostle Paul also states that the man of God must have and maintain a good name, committed to his one wife and her only: "A bishop then must be blameless, the husband of one wife, vigilant, sober, of good behavior, given to hospitality, apt to teach" (1 Timothy 3:2). According to 1 Timothy 3:3, the man of God should not indulge in wine or strong drink. He should not be double-minded but rather sober-minded. The man of God should be wise with his personal finances as well as the financial and business affairs of the church. The man of God must not be a babe in Christ but be mature and tempered so that he will not be easily enticed by the devil. Pastor Dexter Harris, a great teacher of the Word of God, describes the character of the man of God. He says that he is on the front line, and he leads by example. He leads both in his home and in the house of God. His character must remain solid and strong; he must not "be no more children, tossed to and fro, and carried about with every wind of doctrine" (Ephesians 4:14).

The man of God is to lead and protect both his home and the church. The man of God is the first line of defense in both places—it is his charge to encounter the adversary. Do you remember in Genesis when the serpent came and tricked Eve? Had Adam been in his position as the protector, the serpent wouldn't have been able to entice Eve. This is true whether you believe Adam was right there with her at the time or in another location as the serpent is talking to Eve. Either way, Adam never spoke up or took accountability for his lack of positioning and leadership.

My husband, the man of God, and I never spent a lot of time together prior to getting married. We never lived in the same town, so it was at times difficult to spend time with one another. I think back today and realize we never really had a strong courtship. I knew the man (the flesh), but I didn't know the spirit of the man. In praying for my future husband, I never once asked the Lord to show me his heart. We never took the opportunity to get to know each other in a spiritually mature, intimate way. We never learned each other's likes, dislikes, goals, or dreams for marriage and family even after our engagement. I would say we knew each other on a surface level—he knew I enjoyed going to the hair salon every week, and I knew he enjoyed cooking soul food. Before we were married, I knew I had strong feelings for him and loved him, but I can't say I was in love with him. I don't believe he was in love with me either. But I do believe he was in love with the "idea" of being married. He wanted a wife and family on paper. I knew I heard the Lord's approval for our marriage, and I knew that one day he wanted to pastor his own church. I just didn't know it would happen as fast as it did.

We were married, and two and a half years later he started pastoring. Once again, we didn't get a solid foundation; we didn't have enough time to be watered and to blossom and grow together. The scripture says, "Whoso findeth a wife findeth a good thing, and obtaineth favor from the Lord" (Proverbs 18:22). I was familiar with this specific scripture, but I never imagined how powerful it is. As wives, we must realize the gift we are to our husbands. God chose to create Eve from Adam's rib—a hidden part of his body not seen with the naked eye—I believe because of its function. Think about it, the ribs in the body assist in building the thoracic cavity, which helps in *protecting* the heart and the lungs, *supporting* the frame of the body, and *breathing* normally and blocking foreign objects from entering the airway. Wives, just as mother Eve was taken from the rib to help protect and support Adam, we too should, as a great gospel leader would often refer to his wife as his "secret weapon," be our husbands' "secret weapon." We should assist in protecting his heart and supporting his God-given dreams. His enhancer and biggest prayer leader.

My husband desired to pastor early on in his ministry. His name was in the hat a time or two as a candidate, but it didn't happen until his favor came. And oh, did it happen! I was not ready for such a great task, and honestly neither was he. I don't think he counted up the cost as to what it would take to walk in the position of a pastor. Pastoring is more than just being able to preach, teach, pray, and sing. You definitely need to be anointed in those areas; however, it requires a lot of sacrifice on your part, not to mention your family—especially if you have a young and growing family. I believe that sometimes the home is compromised because it was not properly positioned in the first place. It's always good to be led by the Lord. The Bible says to acknowledge the Lord in all your ways and that He would direct our path. Proverbs 3:5-6 states, "Trust in the Lord with all thine heart; and lean not unto thine own understanding. In all thy ways acknowledge him, and he shall direct thy paths." The Bible says that our ways are not His ways, and our thoughts are not His thoughts. That's why we need the Lord to lead us as to what to do, when to do it, how to do it, and where to do it. Isaiah 55:8-9 says, "For my thoughts are not your thoughts, neither are your ways my ways, saith the Lord. For as the heavens are higher than the earth, so are my ways higher than your ways, and my thoughts than your thoughts."

    The man of God must know that just because he has been called or anointed to preach doesn't mean he has been called to be a pastor. "For the vision is yet for the appointed time; It hastens toward the goal and it will not fail, for it will certainly come and not delay" (Habakkuk 2:3). The man of God must know that timing with God is imperative. Lest we consider the Old Testament patriarch, King David, a man after God's own heart. King David is a significant figure in the Bible, and he had experienced and was confronted with controversial issues that many pastors face today. I learned about King David's trauma under the tutelage of Pastor E. Melvin. He dissected in great detail David's story, so much that I couldn't help but correlate David's journey to that of a modern-day spiritual leader or pastor. His story parallels modern day leaders who refuse to deal with their internal ills that cause them to be exposed. Their refusal of personal accountability and integrity causes limited ministerial influence and prevents God from using them in the manner that He desires. King David grew up tending to sheep, and the people of God are referred to as sheep in God's eyes. King David was a gifted musician and didn't mind allowing the Lord to use him to bless others. King David was a warrior and one of the greatest kings in history.

But in 2 Samuel, the Bible breaks down a certain period in King David's life where his timing with God was off, and for that, he sacrificed a lot. David was a man afflicted by issues he refused to deal with, and he loved the praises of the people. He was favored by God, but because he refused to deal with himself, he began to make desperate decisions that just didn't make sense. In 1 Chronicles 28:3, King David wanted to build the Lord a temple. But the Lord says, "You shall not build a house for my name, because you have been a man of war and have shed blood." Let's take a closer look at the comparison of King David and modern-day preachers with internal unresolved issues.

Like King David, the man of God wants to be loved by everyone and hear the praises of the people. In 2 Samuel 7, God gave King David a time to rest, but King David did not take advantage of it. He decided he didn't want to take the opportunity to rest, but once again he talked about building the Lord a house.

Often, the man of God is so busy he neglects spending the proper time with God to get himself or his affairs in order, and this too may cause him to revisit a test more than once. Oftentimes, the man of God prefers not to sit and self-reflect, thinking that the position he has exempts him from having issues, let alone issues he needs to deal with. In chapter 8, King David was proven to be an influential king—the Lord was with him, and he won many battles. The Lord will be with the man of God whom He has called and will bless his ministry. The man of God may even be known all over the world, but that doesn't mean he is successful in God's eyes. There is a difference between having success and being successful. In 2 Samuel 9, King David still refused to address his inner ills, instead deflecting and continuing to focus on helping others. Like so many men of God, they would much rather help others and forsake their own family.

In 2 Samuel 10, King David started fighting again, and this time he made a spectacle of himself. Pastor E. Melvin says it like this: "Those who have the most trauma love to deal in drama." They will do anything not to deal with the "man in the mirror." Chaos will follow anyone who is confused and chooses not to rid themselves of the chaos. The devil loves to lead you away from the will of God as this causes you to be impaired in seeing and hearing from God properly. The devil desires to have the man of God busy, deceived into thinking he is working for the kingdom of God, but in all actuality, he is in his flesh. When he thinks that just because he is at church doing busy church work all hours of the night that he is doing well, but he heard the Lord say, *Go home* hours before.

In 2 Samuel 11, King David was somewhere he shouldn't have been, doing something he shouldn't have been doing. He should have been out fighting, but instead he was home on the roof. It's important for the man of God to walk in integrity. In practicality, he should be where he is supposed to be and doing what he should be doing. There are blessings in obedience and punishments in disobedience! King David was entangled in multiple sins in 2 Samuel. His continual refusal to address his issues caused great harm to him and his family. It is after King David's consequences for his sinful behavior that he is shattered.

The sins that King David committed in 2 Samuel 11 demonstrates how he continually concealed his true reflection in the Word of God. It is after David is shattered that he pens Psalm 51. If you have read Psalm 51 before but were not aware of the meaning behind it and the depth of David's repentance, consider that now as you read:

> Have mercy upon me, O God, according to thy lovingkindness: according unto the multitude of thy tender mercies blot out my transgressions.
>
> Wash me throughly from mine iniquity, and cleanse me from my sin.
>
> For I acknowledge my transgressions: and my sin is ever before me.
>
> Against thee, thee only, have I sinned, and done this evil in thy sight: that thou mightest

be justified when thou speakest, and be clear when thou judgest.

Behold, I was shapen in iniquity; and in sin did my mother conceive me.

Behold, thou desirest truth in the inward parts: and in the hidden part thou shalt make me to know wisdom.

Purge me with hyssop, and I shall be clean: wash me, and I shall be whiter than snow.

Make me to hear joy and gladness; that the bones which thou hast broken may rejoice.

Hide thy face from my sins, and blot out all mine iniquities.

Create in me a clean heart, O God; and renew a right spirit within me.

Cast me not away from thy presence; and take not thy holy spirit from me.

Restore unto me the joy of thy salvation; and uphold me with thy free spirit.

Then will I teach transgressors thy ways; and sinners shall be converted unto thee.

Deliver me from bloodguiltiness, O God, thou God of my salvation: and my tongue shall sing aloud of thy righteousness.

O Lord, open thou my lips; and my mouth shall shew forth thy praise.

> For thou desirest not sacrifice; else would I give it: thou delightest not in burnt offering.
>
> The sacrifices of God are a broken spirit: a broken and a contrite heart, O God, thou wilt not despise.
>
> Do good in thy good pleasure unto Zion: build thou the walls of Jerusalem.
>
> Then shalt thou be pleased with the sacrifices of righteousness, with burnt offering and whole burnt offering: then shall they offer bullocks upon thine altar.

David suffered tremendously for his sins to the point where his family was included in his reaping. Further reading in the book of 2 Samuel 13 reveals several tragedies King David faced. His son Ammon raped his sister Tamar, and David did nothing. Murder, rage, envy, and bitterness were a few of the consequences to King David's actions that tore his family apart. And it affected the kingdom that he ruled as well. David's son Absalom's behaviors were a direct result of what can and did happen in a home where the father is out of place with God. In the end, King David repented of his wrongdoings, including his adulterous behavior with Bathsheba.

Let's explore true repentance. *Repentance,* according to the Oxford Dictionary, is to express or discern sincere regret or guilt for one's wrongdoings or sin. As King David finally saw himself and recognized his sin, he became deeply sorrowful. Second Corinthians 7:10 states, "Godly sorrow brings repentance that leads to salvation." Just saying, "I'm sorry" or "forgive me" is not repentance. True repentance is shown in one's actions. You sincerely regret the sin(s) you committed toward God and man, and a change can be seen in your behavior. There are three primary stages to repentance that many have found valuable when holding others accountable:

1. Acknowledge the sin.
2. Be remorseful.
3. Determine to never commit such act again.

If you ask for forgiveness or say you're sorry, and you know you are sorry only because you were exposed, or if you have not experienced any of the three steps, you have not truly repented. Your ways and desires *must* change.

Many parishioners don't consider the reality of the pastor, nor do they consider what he has been assigned to do. In the last few years, the title and position of "pastor" has been negatively glamorized on television and other platforms. Like many other jobs, you don't really understand the role until you walk therein. In 1 Peter 5:2-4, the Bible instructs the pastor to "Feed the flock of God which is among you, taking the oversight thereof, not by constraint, but willingly; not for filthy lucre, but of a ready mind; neither as being lords over God's heritage, but being ensamples to the flock. And when the Chief Shepherd shall appear, ye shall receive a crown of glory that fadeth not away." There are so many scriptures that give commendation to the office of the pastor on how he should behave and live. I do believe my husband had all good intentions from the start. He wanted to go into the church and build on the foundation that was already laid by his predecessors. He was young and energetic—he believed he could bring a freshness to the ministry. He was also grateful to have been chosen to lead the people of God in the ways of holiness. The truth is, when my husband became the pastor of this church, we were taken there and dropped off. He had no real mentorship or accountability. Every pastor needs a pastor. When the man of God shows signs of weakness or timidity in his pastoral role and loses the respect and esteem of the pastoral position, the journey becomes extremely difficult. The only way to continue effectively is for the Lord to intervene.

The man of God should always remember that he has been called by the Lord and not the people. According to 2 Timothy 4:2, the man of God is commissioned to "preach the Word; be instant in season, out of season; reprove, rebuke, exhort with all longsuffering and doctrine." The man of God's ultimate desire is to serve God and His people. The man of God's focus should never be clouded by pleasing the members of the church or showing respect for persons, as Romans 2:11 says, "For there is no respect for persons with God." The man of God must not allow church members to have or keep their ear where they can't properly and completely hear from God. The man of God should never yearn to hear the latest gossip in church over hearing the voice of God in prayer. First Timothy 3:7 states, "Moreover he must have a good report of them which are without; lest he fall into reproach and the snare of the devil." The man of God should not desire to be common or relaxed with his parishioners where respect is lost. The man of God has the responsibility to protect his family at all costs, from any and all forms of disrespect or mistreatment that his family may encounter. The man of God should know that if he doesn't give or show respect to his wife or family, the church will not respect him either.

There may be times when the husband, the man of God, tries to lead the church when things at his home are lacking. At times, he may make it very obvious that the church is his first priority. As wives of ministers, we need to spend time with God in prayer, seeking wisdom to discern when to have the hard conversations with our husbands, especially when we feel his priorities are off or when there are spiritual issues that need to be addressed. We need to listen to His voice and be willing to do exactly what He says to do concerning the situation. Prayer is the key and the only weapon we have to assist us in this battle in helping our husbands remain focused on serving and pleasing God.

Prayer

Father God, I lift up every ministry family. I pray that You will keep a hedge of protection around us as we seek to do Your will. I pray for each member of the family, individually and collectively, that You will get the glory out of our lives. Father, allow Your will to be done. God, You know that the devil desires to steal, kill, and destroy. God, I ask You to raise a standard against him. I thank You that no weapon formed against our families and our homes will prosper. In Jesus' name, amen.

Chapter 5

THE STRANGE WOMAN

Prayer

Father God, I thank You for being mindful of Your people. Father, I thank You for keeping and shielding us. Thank You for being omniscient, an ever-knowing God who knows what we need. Now, God, have Your way in this situation. I lift up and pray for the angel of this house and for the people of God in this ministry. Father, I ask that You forgive and mend the broken hearts. In Jesus' name, amen.

God's Word Concerning the Matter

My son, attend unto my wisdom and bow thine ear to my understanding: that thou mayest regard discretion, and that thy lips may keep knowledge. For the lips of a strange woman, drops as a honeycomb, and her mouth is smoother than oil: but her feet go down to death; her steps take hold on hell. Lest thou shouldest ponder the path of life, her ways are movable, that thou canst not know them. (Proverbs 5:1-6)

Who is the strange woman? I'm glad you asked! The book of Proverbs describes her as a seductress. She may appear sweet to look upon and even possibly to touch. But she is no more than sand that sifts through your hand as the wind blows. She is one with low self-esteem, albeit she is extremely cunning and deceptive. All the ways of the strange woman are unstable. She has no clue of the destruction she triggers, and all her steps lead straight to hell. The strange woman doesn't care who she tramples over, nor does she mind who slides down her paths of peril. All she wants is to imagine for a moment that her end isn't real. The strange woman desires the embrace of anyone who is willing to make the sacrifices that she herself is not willing to make. And though she knows her end, she takes great pleasure in knowing that her companion is willing to allow her to lead them to death and destruction. She is shattered because her hopes are shattered, her confidence has been stolen, and her dreams seem impossible. Her image is utterly and completely ruined because her insides are broken and scarred by self-hate. Though this strange woman did not have a covenant with God, there may be a strange woman today who has broken their covenant with God and believes she has no value and no worth.

In Proverbs 2:16-19, the Bible depicts the strange woman's destiny: "To deliver thee from the strange woman, even from the stranger which flattereth with her words; Which forsake the guide of her youth, And forgetteth the covenant of her God. For her house inclineth unto death, And her paths unto the dead. None that go unto her return again, neither take they hold of the path of life."

The Strange Woman Redeemed

"But whosoever drinketh of the water that I shall give him shall never thirst; but the water that I shall give him shall be in him a well of water springing up into everlasting life. The woman saith unto him, Sir, give me this water, that I thirst not, neither come hither to draw" (John 4:14-15). These scriptures depict the Samaritan woman who was living a worldly lifestyle and at the time sleeping with a man who wasn't her husband. In this parable, Jesus makes a detour to Samaria just to meet this woman at the well and offer salvation to her. Despite her background, where she was from, and how she was living at the time, Jesus inconvenienced Himself just to minister to the woman at the well. Never think that God won't make a detour just for you! That is just like my God, as He did for her and for me, God is able to make all things new. He can pick you up from wherever you are and give you an abundant life. The strange woman is not beyond redemption; God can change her story! Where she is broken, He can make her whole; where she feels worthless, He can tell her or remind her that her price is far above rubies.

Prayer for the Strange Woman

> *Father, in the name of Jesus, I pray for this strange woman. Father, I ask that You heal and deliver her mind. I pray that she will receive deliverance from every curse and stronghold that has her bound. I pray that she will look to You as Lord and Savior of her life. I pray she will see herself through Your eyes and the Word of God. Father, I pray that she will love herself and know that she is enough in You. I pray, oh God, because You said, "Love your enemies, bless them that curse you, do good to them which despitefully use you, and persecute you." I trust You, God! Help, Lord. In Jesus' name, amen.*

His Strange Woman

One night, she entered the small chapel, hoping that I had already left. I had stayed behind after mid-week Bible study, talking to my husband about what time he would be home that night. I wanted to see what his excuse would be this time for coming home late. Suddenly, the strange woman waltzed in, saw me, and quickly walked out as fast as she entered. I wish I could have captured a picture of her face when she saw me standing there talking to my husband. She wasn't the only one surprised

I was still there. Many others remained as well, I believe just to see our interaction. But I left soon after this odd encounter. I did not want to participate in or appear ignorant of Satan devices.

As I reflect, I am reminded of the time I left town to care for my mother. I honestly believe that's when the devil got busy and reared his ugly head. That's when the strange woman, a member of the church, began to show interest in my husband. I did eventually confront him, but in his stubbornness, he denied it. And he accused me of being jealous! Unbelievable. I thought, *I'm not the jealous one. She is. She became possessive of* my *husband. She wanted* my *husband,* my *family, and* my *position.* As time passed, I began to see my husband entertain her advances, smile at her foolishness, and allow her to get close to him. It was at that time that I admit I became jealous—and this jealousy stemmed from him being comfortable with another woman occupying his space and time.

I was confused by all of this. I didn't understand why my husband didn't stop it. It was as if he was in a trance, and I couldn't wake him. This strange woman was attractive, and I couldn't help but wonder why she didn't have her own man. Why did she desire my husband? I was told by two exceptionally reliable sources that that was just her modus operandi (MO)—how she normally behaved or responded. She was unstable, envious of others, and always desiring what someone else had.

This strange woman pretended she was seeking a strong relationship with the Lord. Oh, the deception was real! In actuality, she was seeking my husband's attention and his anointing. But it's only so long that you can pretend, hide, and deceive before your true stripes are shown. Every opportunity to work and volunteer at the church, she took it. She loved coming to church early and leaving late, doing "busy" church work. She took delight in being a pawn for the devil if she could get close to the pastor. This strange woman was definitely a follower, and she allowed the devil to use her. Her self-esteem and self-respect were depleted. She was very cunning; she was able to deceive a few other parishioners into creating roles for her. She was asked to work and assist in administrative duties in the ministry as well as be a key player in many ministry outings. There were at least several other church members who wanted to see the pastor caught in a scandal. Pick up your mouth, you read that right! It's horrible!

Traps were set for my husband, the pastor, and she was the biggest trap of them all. The correct name for these types of parishioners is clergy killers. *Clergy killers* is a term used in a book written by G. Lloyd Rediger, where he describes a particular church that makes it difficult for the pastor(s) to serve in a congregation: a church where a small group of members is disruptive and does their best to destroy the spiritual leadership by creating traps and enticements under extreme pressures. This happens, and I want to encourage you in case you go through this. Please be prayerful, seek God, and know your assignment! The Bible tells us to watch and pray, and there are definite reasons why we should. When any type of wound enters a church such as this, it could destroy the church's very existence. It is critical that you know your purpose and call for the ministry.

A few members from our church were preparing for a dinner event, and of course, the strange woman was on the committee. Instead of everyone from the church being invited, the committee selected few to attend, excluding any children. Well, though I was invited to come, no children were allowed, therefore I was excluded right from the beginning. As a mother, I never lost sight of who I was. I didn't have the luxury of having assistance with my children. So if there was an event both my husband and I were invited to, and children could not attend, I stayed home. So in the case of this dinner, I knew the exclusion was intentional from the beginning. They wanted to ensure I wouldn't be in attendance.

There were other instances during the time of the affair where my husband was catered to and I was excluded. It felt like the church was choosing to side with the strange woman and her antics. It never feels good as a wife, especially as a pastor's wife, when family members or church members overlook you and disrespect you. Not because of a title but simply because of who you are. One of my spiritual mothers told me once, "The members will always choose the pastor over his wife irrespective of the circumstance." That's exactly how I was feeling! Did they not see this craziness? Why were they pretending to be blind? But I had to refocus and spend more time in my war room, praying for not only myself but for the church as well. The strange woman played her role, and in the eyes of the clergy killers, she should have been given an Oscar for her performance. However, let me be very clear: I do not blame or fault her or anyone else for my husband's behavior and actions. I hold him completely responsible. He chose to listen to, cater to, and spend time with the strange woman. He made the choice.

The Lord revealed so much to me concerning this affair, including all who were involved in its facilitation. I knew who set up appointments, who initiated church outings, who drove by various hotels, who took pictures, and the list goes on. No one else is to blame, although others did participate in ensuring all the right traps were secured for this illicit affair with the pastor and this strange woman. Wife, because of who you are and because the favor of God rests upon you, the Lord will not have you blinded by the works of the devil—and I appreciate this gift of discernment.

According to 1 Corinthians 2:10-11, "These are the things God has revealed to us by his Spirit. The Spirit searches all things, even the deep things of God. For who knows a person's thoughts except for their own spirit within them? In the same way, no one knows the thoughts of God except the Spirit of God." The Holy Spirit gives the believer revelation knowledge. In many instances the Holy Spirit will instruct the believer on what to do and just how to do it. During this time, I was faced with a lot of uncertainty, and I constantly second-guessed myself. If I didn't know God's voice, I would have lost my mind. There would be times when the Lord would reveal things to me, and my husband would not believe it was the leading of the Lord. I must admit I would be amazed at times. I am grateful to be attuned to the Holy Spirit. I prefer to deal with life circumstances head-on with the help of the Lord! There are many things I have experienced, and I have suffered through trials and circumstances that didn't feel good or look good.

The Word of God in Romans 8:28, declares, "And we know that all things work together for good to them that love God, to them who are the called according to his purpose." So I know that if God is with me, no matter what I'm facing, in the end it will work for my good.

Can we give this strange woman a name? For scriptural purposes, let's call her Delilah. Delilah means amorous. The word *amorous,* according to dictionary. com, means showing, feeling, or related to sexual desire. The Hebrew meaning of *Delilah* is small or lacking wealth. Delilah, in Judges 16, was a seductress. Delilah was Samson's lover who inadvertently destroyed his life. Delilah was convinced to seduce Samson and discern the secret of his angelic strength. Delilah obliged in an effort to satisfy her sexual appetite and to assure her financial security.

The Philistines were threatened by Samson and wanted him dead. Delilah was a Philistine and Samson a Nazirite. Nazirites were set apart for the service of God. Samson was dedicated to God before his birth. His hair represented his strength and was a sign that God was with him. Judges 13:2-5 states,

> A certain man of Zorah, named Manoah, from the clan of the Danites, had a wife who was childless, unable to give birth. The angel of the Lord appeared to her and said, "You are barren and childless, but you are going to become pregnant and give birth to a son. Now see to that you drink no wine or other fermented drink and that you do not eat anything unclean. You will become pregnant

and have a son whose head is never to be touched by a razor because the boy is to be a Nazarite, dedicated to God from the womb."

Samson was considered to be one of the strongest men of his time. Yet he was weakened by the words of a seductress harlot. After multiple intimate encounters with Samson, Delilah managed to entangle him in her deceptive web. Delilah not only granted the request of the Philistines, but she satisfied her own craving. Samson allowed Delilah to destroy him through his own lust and his unwillingness to stay committed to God. Delilah was a skilled wanton—having many casual relationships—and Samson fell right into her arms. Sound familiar? Samson was intoxicated by Delilah, but he had no idea that this relationship would destroy everything he loved and valued.

Conclusion

According to Merriam-Webster, *strange* is something unfamiliar or different from the norm. It's safe to say that Delilah definitely lived up to the description of a strange woman. I would like to explore the modern-day Delilah. We have all read, seen, and heard of women who persist in damaging the credibility and character of pastors, presidents, or any man in a powerful position of authority. Oh, these women love prominent men. This is not new, nor should it be recognized as normal. Attempting to understand the strange woman, I discovered that ninety percent of single women only desire to seek after married men. This term is called *mate poaching. Psychology Today* defines mate poaching as having interest to romantically entice someone who is currently involved with another person, be it through marital status or just dating. They also suggest that both men and women believe the grass is greener on the other side. Picking the lock to the fence and walking on the well-manicured lawn is a treat for the strange woman.[4] To her, the man is seen as a good catch—he is already cleaned up and trained, and he appears to be settled and committed.

There are several reasons why a single woman may want a married man:

- No commitment. Yes, she does not see commitment as most do. This woman wants her man to be committed and loyal to her, but she holds no commitment to anyone. She desires personal space and privacy and the freedom to do her own thing with whomever she chooses.
- The secrecy of the relationship. This woman enjoys the rush that the secrecy of the relationship provides. Sneaking around is more pleasurable than commitment. Luring the man is not the problem; she must have a "certain kind of man" that motivates her.
- Competition. She likes competition. She likes to compete; this builds her low self-esteem. She loves to feel superior to the wife. Wanting this man to desire her more than his wife is a game that she *thinks* she has mastered. I am convinced

---

4. Martin Graff, "Mate Poaching: Are Friends a Threat," *Psychology Today* (2022), https://www.psychologytoday.com/us/blog/love-digitally/202009/mate-poaching-are-friends-threat.

that the modern-day Delilah is very similar to the Delilah from the Bible. She wants what she wants and will use her physical attractiveness to get just that.

Words of Wisdom

In the last chapter, I gave wisdom to the man of God. Please allow me to offer some words of wisdom to men in general:

- Be careful whose lap you lay your head in. Proverbs 5:3-4 states, "For the lips of a strange woman drop as a honeycomb, And her mouth is smoother than oil: but her end is bitter as wormwood, Sharp as a two-edged sword." Be mindful of who you let rub your head and speak into your ear. The touch may be ever so soothing, but you find yourself awakened to your demise.
- Be careful of a woman who wants to bring you down and not help build you up. Proverbs 5:6 (NLT) says, "For she cares nothing about the path to life. She staggers down a crooked trail and doesn't realize it." Not every woman knows her purpose in life or how to pursue that purpose. She may not have the ability to support you walking in your calling.
- Be committed to having and keeping values. First Kings 21:25 (NLT) says, "No one else so completely sold himself to what was evil in the Lord's sight as Ahab did under the influence of his wife Jezebel." In this text, Ahab allowed a

woman who happens to be his wife to influence him in wickedness. Man, I implore you to stand strong on what is right; be the head and king God created you to be in every situation.
- Remember, two minutes of pleasure can lead to death—whether naturally, spiritually, or both. Proverbs 23:27-28 (NLT) states, "A prostitute is a dangerous trap; a promiscuous woman is as dangerous as falling into a narrow well. She hides and waits like a robber, eager to make more men unfaithful." Stay woke!
- Women typically react faster than men. Judges 16:13-18 states,

> And Delilah said unto Samson, Hitherto thou hast mocked me, and told me lies: tell me wherewith thou mightiest be bound. And he said unto her, if thou weavest the seven locks of my head with the web. And she fastened it with the pin, and said unto him, The Philistines be upon thee, Samson. And he awaked out of his sleep, and went away with the pin of the beam, and with the web. And she said unto him, how canst thou say, I love thee, when thine heart is not with me? Thou hast mocked me these three times, and hast not told me wherein thy great strength lieth. And it came to pass, when she pressed him daily with her words, and urged him so that

his soul was vexed unto death; that he told her all his heart, and said unto her, There hath not come a razor upon mine head; for I have been a Nazarite unto God from my mother's womb: if I be shaven, then my strength will go from me, and I shall become weak, and be like any other man.

"There is therefore now no condemnation to them which are in Christ Jesus, who walk not after the flesh, but after the Spirit" (Romans 8:1). Strange woman, you too can be healed, delivered, and made whole. Allow God to change your name! We don't have to remain sick, sinful, or diseased. You can be transformed and redeemed by surrendering to the Lord. Allow God to take charge of your life. There is nothing too hard for God— let your yesterday be your past and today be your new walk in Christ. Let the Lord strengthen you to walk in your calling.

Prayer

Father God, thank You. Thank You for being Jehovah Nissi, our banner over us. You knew about this affair before the characters, the scene, or the actions were conceived in their minds and hearts. You foreknew the scars and the bruises it would cause and every life that would be affected. You led us through the valley of the shadow of death, and for that alone again, I say, thank You. I will never understand why *it had to be this way,* why *this path was chosen. This song is so true: "If I were in control of my life, I would have worked things out much differently, there would be no hurts, no pains." I am learning that the chosen path You have for Your children is not pain free or without bumps and winding roads. As I continue to lift up my husband, our church, and our ministry, I will remain submissive. I will always seek Your will. I will prayerfully follow Your guidance on this journey called life. Amen.*

Chapter 6

FAITHFULLY SHELTERED

"The Lord is faithful to ALL His promises and loving toward ALL He has made." (Psalms 145:13)

Meditation

My God, my Yahweh Sabaoth, my watchful defender: You have always been and are my shelter in the midst of all of my storms. God, You have been my strength in weakness. You have been and are my peace, even when everything around me is chaotic. You are my peace of mind when my mind grows weary. God, even when the enemy comes in like a tsunami, You and only You can lift a standard against him and make everything calm. God, I thank You for lifting a standard against the enemies in my life. I have not only seen Your presence, but I have experienced Your presence calming the vicious winds and waves in my

> life. My enemies were allowed to prepare a table that I feasted upon. I have witnessed multiple times how You have allowed my enemies to sit as my footstool, while You, God, lifted me up. You have been faithful to me and Your Word. I will always be thankful and will give You praise all the days of my life.

When you have been through hell and back and know that it was only by the grace of God that you survived without being crazy, you learn not to sweat the small stuff. You learn not to care about what other people think. You learn not to feel rejected when others don't like you. You learn to be OK when others abandon you. You even learn to be OK when others disrespect you and ignore the anointed treasure you are. You respectfully become unbothered by those who cannot handle your vision(s), and you get over those who cannot understand or respect your boundaries. When you have suffered and have been crushed for your oil, your attitude changes. Your attachment to people and things also changes. Superficiality and inauthenticity are no longer tolerable. You stop feeling like you must be a certain way to be accepted. Your discernment changes, and your patience for foolishness dwindles. Your willingness to be silent and tolerant of abusive behavior also shifts. *Lord, I am forever grateful for Your sheltering.*

Prayer

Father God, I come before Your throne, asking for strength and wisdom. Thank You, Lord, for being there when I need You. I bless You for comforting, guiding, and allowing me to cry out to You. There are circumstances that I am experiencing that I don't for the life of me understand. I feel weak, worn, and helpless. Father, I seek Your shelter, where I know I can find safety and rest in Your shadow. I thank You for being my fortress and my shield. Although I don't understand, I trust Your wisdom and Your strength to endure this trial. I know this will bring You glory. In Jesus' name, amen.

For those of you going through an incredibly hard time and are growing weary . . . for those of you who are wrestling with the darkness that may feel overwhelming—don't allow it to penetrate your heart. Remember that you have an inheritance in Christ. Rest assured that in due time, trouble will fade, and God's light of love will forever shine in your life. Whatever happens, remember not to lose hope. Hold on to Jesus, who is always present and unchanging.

In this chapter, I want to demonstrate how, through the power of God's Word and through intense prayer, God sheltered me. I had to faithfully allow God to shelter me. God will be whatever you need Him to be, but we must accept Him and allow Him to be. When you are aware of the plans of the enemy because the Lord has given you insight, this insight alters the impact of the enemy's plan. God is good!

We must remember that the enemy is always on assignment: "The devil prowls around like a roaring lion, looking for someone to devour" (1 Peter 5:8). Our awareness of what the enemy is planning and knowing his assignment in our lives places us in a position of victor. If we didn't have purpose on this earth, promises from God, and power to resist the devil, the devil would not give us a second thought. The devil is after our surrender! The devil desires for us to forfeit our race, throw in the towel, and ultimately give up on God.

The Bible declares in Psalms 25:1-5,

> Unto thee, O Lord, do I lift up my soul. O my God, I trust in thee: Let me not be ashamed, let not mine enemies' triumph over me. Yea, let none that wait on thee be ashamed: Let them be ashamed which transgress without cause. Shew me thy ways, O Lord; Teach me thy paths. Lead me in thy truth and teach me: For thou art the God of my salvation; on thee do I wait all the day.

The scriptures gave me life and continue to be part of my spiritual weaponry.

God cares about us and everything that concerns us. In 1 Peter 5:7 it says, "Casting all your care upon him; for he careth for you." The Lord wants us to know that He is touched by what touches us. He feels our infirmities. God allows our tests, and He guides our trials. In the midst of my suffering, I heard the Lord say,

I care. Often we don't give our cares to the Lord. Yet we get frustrated and aggravated when the situation doesn't change. We find ourselves talking about the matter but refusing to release it to God. *Release it to God.* The Lord said to me, and I'm saying to you, that He wants our problems, cares, hurts, and pains. He says, "Cast them on Me, for I care for you. Release those worries, and I will handle it for you!"

Prayer

> *Lord, I thank You for being concerned about me. I'm grateful that I'm learning to cast my cares on You. I trust You with my heart and know that You will heal the hurt. Thank You for being mindful of me. In Jesus' name, amen.*

I learned to press beyond how I felt and what I saw. There is blessing in pressing. I recognized that the enemy is always working to cause me to faint. Satan knows that if I make up my mind, it's over! If I can keep my mind on Jesus and stay focused on God's promises, I will defeat the enemy. Satan will not get the victory. In the Bible, God told the children of Israel that they would be victorious, but to manifest that victory, they would have to march around the walls of Jericho in silence. God didn't want them to talk, He didn't want them to attack, He didn't want them to complain. He wanted them to silently march. During this season of my life, I had to learn to be quiet, to not mumble, and to refrain from arguments with my husband. I couldn't complain to anyone. I had to keep moving and marching in the things of God. I had to keep being faithful, keep moving forward in ministry, keep fasting and praying. I eventually learned that faith was not required for me to keep marching in the things of God. It took great faith for me to be quiet and trust God. It took faith not to complain or fight with my husband. God was showing me how to study to be quiet and walk in faith and not by sight. So I quietly sat in service, participated in ministry, and showed the love of God to my enemies. I showed God's love to those who I knew were whispering behind my back. I had to trust in the assurance that God had me covered.

Prayer

> *Father God, You declare in Your Word, "For we walk by faith, and not by sight." Thank You for giving me a measure of faith. There were times that You gave me faith to gaze upon You, listen to You, and trust You with every step I took. Thank You for helping me to be quiet and get out of my own way. In Jesus' name, amen.*

My special time with the Lord is at midnight. In prayer one night, Isaiah 48:10 came to my mind. I quickly grabbed the Bible and began to read: "Behold, I have refined thee, but not with silver; I have chosen thee in the furnace of affliction." I've learned through my struggles and in life that the promises of God are free, but the oil will cost you. The oil from the promises of God will equip you to elevate to new levels. You will be equipped to do battle with greater devils and walk through fires that would have normally burned you to death. But because of the sheltering of God, I have come through this test. To God be the glory. In times of trouble, look to God. His unfailing love is enough.

Many chapters in the book of Psalms helped me as I would cry out to God. I search the Word for inspiration and to gain deeper revelation. There was one time in particular I found multiple chapters that described what I was feeling, thinking, and wanting to say. I found treasures in the words, and I wanted them to manifest in my life. I read Psalms 27 through 42. I was in deep despair and only found solace in God's Word. It was in the Word where I found hope. The Word of God helped alter my mind to a mindset to praise, despite what I was facing. The book of Psalms speaks to the hurting, the anguished, and the lonely. In my opinion, the book of Psalms soothes you during difficult trials. The psalmist's messages to readers can change you. It helps pull you out of depression. It encourages you to endure and hold fast to the promises of God.

Declaring the truth of scripture brings power to the earth. The Word of God is so powerful—it is both encouraging and inspiring. I want to encourage you: when you are overwhelmed by the stresses of life, when you feel hopeless and helpless, turn to the Word. I recommend the book of Psalms for uplifting, renewal, revival, and restoration. Reading about God's love and faithfulness to His children can bring hope and increase trust. God's

Word is the only thing that abides forever; it is unfailing, and it is unchanging. God's Word can literally raise the dead. Let God resurrect you through His Word.

One night, my husband and I joined together in prayer, and I remember it like it was yesterday:

Closing Prayer

> *Father God, in the name of Jesus we thank You for this time and opportunity tonight to come before You in prayer. God, we lift up our marriage. Lord, we thank You for the thirty-plus years You have been with us. Thank You for being mindful of us and blessing us in spite of our failures. Thank You for not leaving or forsaking us. Thank You, God, for loving us even when we have been in our flesh. Forgive us for being selfish, forgive us for being stubborn, forgive us for not obeying Your Word. Forgive us for not putting You first and allowing You to order our steps! Lord, help us to be intentional in the things of God. Help us to be mindful and respectful at all times to one another. Do what needs to be done for us individually and together. God, do it so You may get the glory out of this marriage. Bind the hand of the devil. Loose love, honor, and respect in each of us. In Jesus' mighty name, amen.*

www.ingramcontent.com/pod-product-compliance
Lightning Source LLC
Chambersburg PA
CBHW071738090426
42738CB00011B/2517